Many have written before about the tragedy of Christian organisations losing what the authors call 'organisational faithfulness', but few have offered such practical advice on how to avoid it! This long-overdue book is a must-read for trustees, executives, employees and supporters of Christian organisations, wishing to remain true to their founders' missions.

Professor Kenneth J. Barnes

Mockler-Phillips Chair in Workplace Theology and Business Ethics, Gordon-Conwell Theological Seminary

As the CEO of a large Christian organisation – World Vision Australia – I believed we would only flourish organisationally if we struggled with the question of organisational faithfulness. The Apostle Paul talks about something that is supra personal or supra individual in his language of 'powers and principalities'. I wish I had access to this book when I was a CEO and welcome such a refreshing and thoughtful resource.

Rev. Tim Costello

Former CEO of World Vision Australia

Keeping Faith *is a project long overdue, challenging the expectation of organisational drift with a new and important approach they call 'organisational faithfulness'. Like all brilliant ideas, once you read about organisational faithfulness, it sounds too obvious to have been missed. But it has been missed. And I pray that* Keeping Faith *becomes the go-to guide for maintaining Christian faithfulness in every kind of organisation that claims to honour Jesus Christ.*

Dr John Dickson

Historian, author and Jean Kvamme Distinguished Professor at Wheaton College (Illinois)

Christians are called to be signs and sacraments of God's presence in the world as well as in the Church. This book will help to inform and inspire the everyday faith of those who are concerned to influence the corporate culture of their organisations and who seek to embody gospel values in the public square.

Canon Professor Elaine Graham

Professor Emerita, University of Chester

From Harvard to the YMCA, organizations have drifted from their founding Christian mission. Keeping Faith *is a timely and important book that thoughtfully explores why our organizations need not only to do good work, but also to remain faithful. In an era of both subtle and overt pulls toward secularisation, we need courageous leaders who avoid the well-worn path of mission drift and faithfully pursue the narrow way of implementing their full mission.* Keeping Faith *prompts readers to pay careful attention, align beliefs and actions, and avoid subtle compromises that threaten their convictions. This book will help us be found faithful.*

Peter Greer
President and CEO of HOPE International and co-author of *Mission Drift*

I wish as a CEO and leader in Christian organisations I could have read this book before I started. I wish I could have given it to my senior leaders and especially intending board members. Our biggest risk in Christian organisations is not financial, nor operational. It is failing to deliver on our calling as an organisation. This often happens because the call is clear, but we don't have a system of theology that keeps us true to that call. This leads to what we call mission drift and in too many cases mission is completely lost. The authors have at last articulated a model that can stop this happening – stop this failure – and help us stay true to Christ in our work. I highly recommend you read it, answer the questions and work out how to implement this in your organisation.

Toby Hall
Former CEO of St Vincent's Health Australia, and Mission Australia

The significance of this subject for all Christian organisations can hardly be over-rated. How often the vision and ideals of the founders are not sustained by those who succeed them! We certainly need to consider the matter frequently and thoughtfully. This challenging book provokes us to think, pray and dialogue about the issues as we guard the good deposit which has been given to us.

Archbishop Dr Peter Jensen
Archbishop of the Anglican Diocese of Sydney 2001–2013,
founding General Secretary of GAFCON

Organisational faithfulness may be the hardest work a Christian organisation ever does and resources to assist in the rigorous thinking and theological reflection necessary to maintain this are scarce. That this book provides deeply reflective questions that provoke equally practical actions is rarer still. Even as someone entirely committed to the ideals that Keeping Faith *espouses, this book challenged and convicted me that there is much more to reflect on, to articulate, and to embed. It will prove a valuable and overdue resource and I look forward to the continued challenge and kingdom impact it will bring.*

Melissa Lipsett
CEO of Baptist World Aid Australia

This book is an indispensable guide for leaders and board members of Christian schools, social service organisations, international development organisations and hospitals who will have to stand before God and account for the faithfulness of their organisations. No question is more important for Christian mission in Australia over the next few years than this faithfulness.

Paul Oslington
Professor of Economics and Theology, Alphacrucis University College

This is a vibrating book. It emits the constant vibe that the authors know what they are talking about. Here is the counsel, challenge, and guidance of practitioners long experienced in the high calling of running Christian organisations. Not far into my reading of the book, I concluded that every Board member of every Christian organisation should devour this book: they will find both inspiration and warning here. As I read on, I found myself thinking every CEO and senior staff member of Christian organisations should read this book: it will empower them to act out their faith in grace-filled treatment of employees. Still less than half-way through, I was convinced that every staff member of a Christian organisation on recruitment should be presented with this book: it will enable them to be confident about what to expect and what is expected of them.

Dr Stuart Piggin
Conjoint Associate Professor of History, Macquarie University

Christians have a long history of establishing schools, hospitals, agencies of community care and support and other benevolent institutions to serve the world in the name of Jesus. Though some of these institutions have enjoyed great success and become household names, not all have been able to maintain their Christian focus and purpose, their 'first love'. Others struggle to see the personal Christian commitment of leaders, staff and board members permeate the warp and weft of the way the organisation operates. Full of thoughtful reflection on key biblical principles and drawing on extensive and diverse experience of leading and studying organisations, this is a volume to stimulate intentional reflection (including a discussion guide) on the enduring Christian shape of an organisation's ethos, identity and impact. I warmly commend this volume to boards and staff teams, and all those who have a concern for Christian organisations seeking to serve the gospel in the world at large, a pressing and vital challenge.

Archbishop Kanishka Raffel
Anglican Archbishop of Sydney

Organisational leaders have long known that culture trumps strategy. When it comes to mission drift, or more accurately, theology drift, it is also true that the theology an organisation affirms is of no value unless it embodies that theology. Keeping Faith is a brilliant diagnostic tool for analysing organisational theology and shows how organisations can remain faithful. Practical theology at its best, this book is a gift to any leader who longs to promote a gospel-infused culture in the organisation they lead.

Dr Brian Rosner
Principal, Ridley College, Melbourne

Faithfully leading organisations to hold true to their founding call to demonstrate God's love in action is not simple. It's hard. Many have failed. This important book charts a clear roadmap to inspire belief in God's work in organisations and hope that his redemption of the world will prevail as he liberates his mission through teams. It is essential reading for all Christian leaders and anyone who seeks to explore the vital role organisations can have in changing the world.

Donna Shepherd
Chair, World Vision International

Keeping Faith *raises the difficult question of how Christian organisations remain faithful to serving God's mission throughout the world. I am thankful that Judd, Swinton and Martin, have tackled such a relevant topic for all Christian organisations. The stories and sometimes failures that they share invite the reader to learn alongside the authors as they tackle the difficult issues that can hinder Christian organisations; from the Christian 'nice' culture to the slow drift of organisational mission.*

Clare Steele
CEO of Compassion Australia

Keeping Faith *articulates a beautiful organisational theology that resists the temptation to go Jesus-lite in Christian organisations in order to satisfy secular metrics. Not content with statements of doctrine or values alone, Judd, Swinton and Martin argue convincingly for forms of organisational discipleship where theology is embedded in questions of identity, aim, behaviour and impact. The temptations of perpetual busyness, estrangement from theology and the church, and mission drift for the sake of funding, are articulated with wisdom. A summons to think about how belief becomes faithful corporate practice, presses for organisational conversion in the service of Christ! What a challenging, refreshing and timely book!*

Revd Dr Richard R. Topping
President and Vice-Chancellor, Vancouver School of Theology

KEEPING
FAITH

How Christian
organisations can
stay true to
the way of Jesus

Stephen Judd
John Swinton
Kara Martin

Langham
GLOBAL LIBRARY

© 2023 Stephen Judd, John Swinton and Kara Martin

Published 2024 by Langham Global Library
An imprint of Langham Publishing
www.langhampublishing.org

Langham Publishing and its imprints are a ministry of Langham Partnership

Langham Partnership
PO Box 296, Carlisle, Cumbria, CA3 9WZ, UK
www.langham.org

First published in 2023 by Acorn Press, an imprint of Bible Society Australia.

This edition:

ISBNs:
978-1-78641-035-1 Print
978-1-78641-067-2 ePub
978-1-78641-068-9 PDF

Unless otherwise indicated, Scripture quotations are taken from the Holy Bible, New International Version® Anglicised, NIV® Copyright © 1979, 1984, 2011 by Biblica, Inc.® Used by permission. All rights reserved worldwide.

British Library Cataloguing-in-Publication Data
A catalogue record for this book is available from the British Library

ISBN: 978-1-78641-035-1

Edited by Kristin Argall
Cover and text design and layout by John Healy

Contents

About the authors

Dr Stephen Judd is the former Chief Executive of HammondCare – an Australian Christian independent charitable trust working within health and aged-care provision and with an annual turnover of over $A400m.

Professor John Swinton is a Scottish theologian based at the University of Aberdeen in Scotland, United Kingdom. He was Chaplain to Queen Elizabeth II of England and is now Chaplain to King Charles III.

Kara Martin, Adjunct Professor at Gordon-Conwell Theological Seminary, is a practical theologian and author/editor of three books dealing with faith–work.

PREFACE

The loss of faithfulness

We can all think of organisations that were established by Christians that are no longer Christian. George Marsden's *The Soul of the American University* and James Burtchaell's *The Dying of the Light* are two works that meticulously chronicle what Marsden calls the transition from religious establishment to *established non-belief* within American educational institutions.[1] They detail how mottos and logos change, such as Harvard's 'Veritas Christo et Ecclesia' (Truth for Christ and Church) to the 'glittering generality' of 'Veritas'.[2] They describe in excruciating detail how doctrinal enquiry is gradually avoided because it is divisive, as if tertiary institutions are too fragile an environment for contested ideas. In published documents the words and deeds of Jesus are replaced with a 'vapid humanism', and over time, boards have fewer ministers of religion as trustees and, then, even fewer trustees who are worshippers at any church.[3]

Elsewhere, the Young Men's Christian Association (YMCA) was established by George Williams in mid-nineteenth-century England to improve 'the spiritual condition' of young men in the slums of London. Originally the YMCA focused on Bible studies and prayer meetings and 'mutual improvement societies'. By the 1880s, it had crossed the Atlantic to the United States and had become a missionary organisation, commissioning over 20,000 missionaries to evangelise the world. However, following World War I the evangelistic zeal of the YMCA waned and revenues declined. Bible studies were

---

1 Marsden, *The Soul of the American University*; Burtchaell, *The Dying of the Light*.
2 Burtchaell, *The Dying of the Light*, p. 46.
3 Ibid., pp. 37, 39.

dropped in favour of a focus on fitness. Almost inevitably, the YMCA soon secularised the story of its founder and rebranded to become the inoffensive and nondescript 'Y'.[4]

A similar story can be told about Australia's Benevolent Society, which was established in 1813 as the 'NSW Society for Promoting Christian Knowledge and Benevolence in these Territories and the Neighbouring Islands'. Today the Benevolent Society describes itself as 'the first private charitable organisation dedicated to meeting needs of vulnerable groups in Australian society'.[5] Further, it is keen to assure visitors to its website that 'While [the Benevolent Society's] origins were Christian, it soon went on to become a non-religious, unaffiliated organisation'.[6]

This is not simply a phenomenon of the distant past. Habitat for Humanity was founded in 1976 by Millard Fuller. Towards the end of his life, Fuller said:

> I have a deep concern that Habitat for Humanity remains firmly a
> Christian ministry. From the beginning I have seen Habitat as a new
> frontier in Christian missions – a creative and new way to proclaim
> the gospel ... My greatest concern for Habitat for Humanity is
> going secular.[7]

His fears were well-founded: in 2005 Fuller left Habitat and established the Fuller Centre for Housing. This time, 'Millard was determined that it had to be a return to the grassroots, Christian principles with which he had started Habitat' less than 30 years previously.[8]

In Australia, the Anglican parish of St James' King Street in Sydney established the St James' Ethic Centre in 1989. Thirty years on, it is now known

4 Greer & Horst, *Mission Drift*, pp. 68–69.
5 'Our History', The Benevolent Society, https://www.benevolent.org.au/about-us/our-history, accessed 22 July 2022.
6 Ibid.
7 Greer & Horst, *Mission Drift*, p. 172.
8 The Fuller Center for Housing, n.d., https://fullercenter.org/why-millard-fuller-and-habitat-parted-ways/

as the Ethics Centre, a secular organisation with seemingly no suggestion that its motivation was initially or currently Christian.

And there are many other examples: the secularisation of formerly Christian organisations is a worldwide phenomenon. Says Chris Crane of Edify, a global education aid organisation:

> It's the exception that an organisation stays true to its mission. The natural course – the unfortunate natural evolution of many originally Christ-centered missions – is to drift.[9]

This is a gloomy conclusion. How does it happen? How do Christian organisations become secular? How can you ensure that your organisation is what Crane says is an exception? How do we defend against what he describes as the 'unfortunate natural evolution'? And what should we all be aware of?

These are questions that concern us greatly, and which we will address in this book.

We believe that the most important thing that God requires of Christian organisations is faithfulness to the Christian life: expressed in the Bible and modelled by Jesus. This faithfulness is maintained by ensuring an overlap between the *ethos* (culture, spirit) of an organisation with its Christian *identity* and the *impact* that it has. It is a faithfulness that is informed by a deep and contextual Statement of Organisational Theology.

This book will help you analyse your organisation and lay the foundations for developing a robust organisational theology.

'Now it is required that those who have been given a trust must prove faithful' (1 Cor 4:2).[10]

Stephen Judd, John Swinton and Kara Martin

---

9 Chris Crane, President and CEO of Edify, quoted in Greer & Horst, *Mission Drift*, p. 19. Crane was formerly President and CEO of Opportunity International.
10 Italics added.

Abbreviations

CEO	chief executive officer
CMS-A	Church Missionary Society of Australia
P&C	People and Culture (team)
PPE	personal protective equipment
RSL	Returned and Services League
YMCA	Young Men's Christian Association

The Concept of Organisational Faithfulness

Christian organisations are under fire from external forces: government regulations that privatise faith imperatives, the increasing secularisation of society and economic pressures. As well, they are under fire from within: insufficient employees of faith, employees deconstructing from orthodox faith and the hypocrisy of dualistic practices that breaks employee trust.

Is it possible to have a Christian organisation that remains faithful to the Christian life: expressed in the Bible and modelled by Jesus?

How can Christian leaders navigate the tension between the world of business and the world of faith?

In this section we will attempt to answer those questions from our perspective as three individuals who have straddled the worlds of business, not-for-profits and theological education – with a combined total of 100 years of experience.

1. Is it possible for an organisation to be Christian?

The Bible consists only of stories about religious people and spiritual ideas, right? Not quite. Take the four Gospels: Matthew, Mark, Luke and John, which describe the life of Jesus – they are full of talk about business and ways of organising human productivity. Approximately 60% of Jesus' parables involve business and commerce. They are full of metaphors about business management, modes of productivity and faithful business transactions. Jesus' teaching seems very much geared towards the rhythms and practices of business and organisation, and the impact of such practices on our stewardship of the world.

As we reflect on Jesus' words, it becomes clear that work in general – and the work of business management in particular – are important aspects of faithful participation in God's coming kingdom. In the Gospels, we are urged to

- *purchase* property for a pearl of great worth or a treasure (Matt 13:44–46)
- *cultivate* the land (Mark 4:26–29)
- *sow* seed and *reap* the crops (Matt 13:3–9; Mark 4:3–9; Luke 8:5–8)
- *deal* with the problem of weeds (Matt 13:24–30)
- *face the challenges* of difficult workers (Matt 20:1–16)
- *deal effectively with tenants* who are unjust and unfair (Matt 21:33–41; Mark 12:1–9, Luke 20:9–16).

In his story about the wise and the foolish builders, Jesus even comments on *construction work*, offering some vital advice to those who desire to build robust houses (Luke 6:48–49). Throughout the Gospels, poor business practices and a lack of business acumen are condemned as unjust – and worse, unfaithful (Luke 16:1–13).

The assumption in these stories is not simply about making money for money's sake. Rather, the issue is ensuring that we do *business for God's sake*. Jesus urges us to take the matter of faithfulness in the marketplace very seriously (Matt 25:14–30; Luke 19:12–27). We live in a world that has been gifted to us, and we have been given responsibility to manage, care and tend for God's creation (Gen 1:26–28). Developing businesses and organisations that are oriented towards the goals and intentions of the Creator is of the utmost importance. That responsibility includes the making of profit, the godly use of that profit and the avoidance of unnecessary loss and waste.

Importantly, such responsibility means that our desires for profit, efficiency and growth must be determined by the goals of the kingdom. There is therefore no inherent problem with Christians being involved in organisations that do their work within the realm of business.

Involvement in business and commerce is a complex and challenging endeavour, however. Jesus calls us to be 'as *shrewd* as snakes and as *innocent* as doves' (Matt 10:16, italics added). Holding the tension between these two modes of human action can be challenging, and at times it will run counter to the standard goals of business which are investment return and competitiveness.

Can a business be Christian?

So, what does this mean for businesses that identify as 'Christian'? How exactly can an organisation with Christian intent function within this environment without compromising its values or losing its soul? This question becomes even more complex when we consider that for many organisations, a number, and perhaps even a majority, of its employees are non-Christians. In this book we will answer questions such as these and untangle some of the practical and theological complexities that surround the running of Christian organisations.

It is hoped that by bringing together theology and experience, we will be able to offer important insights into the practices of Christians in business and what it means to function faithfully within an environment that can, at times, be challenging for Christians.

What makes a Christian organisation?

Working out what we mean when we talk about 'Christian organisations' is not as straight forward as we may assume. At one level the answer to the question of whether an organisation can be Christian is a simple 'No!' Organisations can certainly be in the service of God, but does that make them Christian? Perhaps, but we would have to think of the term 'Christian' in quite a different way from the norm.

At the individual level, to be a Christian is to become a follower of Jesus, a disciple, who is then given a vocation to participate with the mission of God. So, in Matthew 28:19–20 Jesus' great commandment is this:

> Therefore go and make disciples of all nations, baptising them in the name of the Father and of the Son and of the Holy Spirit, and teaching them to obey everything I have commanded you. And surely I am with you always, to the very end of the age.

This is a command to help people become Christians. To be a Christian is a personal and a communal way of being in the world. We commit ourselves to Jesus and, in the Spirit, we become members of Jesus' body. In becoming Christians, we recognise who Jesus is, realise that we have become distanced from God, repent, discover grace and salvation, and allow the Spirit to carry out the work of sanctification and redemption.

Importantly, once people decide to follow Jesus, their identity is redefined. Now they are who they are *in Christ* (Gal 2:20). They become one body: the body of Jesus (1 Cor 12:27). Disciples are not defined by what they have done, can do or will be in the future. They are not defined by the efficacy of any organisational structures, including the church which is inevitably human and flawed. They are defined as people who live in and for Christ; a people who live in a community that is quite literally the body of Jesus.

There is clearly a corporate dimension to being Christian. It is, however, very different from the corporate identity that sits at the heart of any organisation, including those who claim the moniker 'Christian'. It is difficult to see how any humanly created organisation could be classified as Christian according to these criteria. So, what do we mean when we call an organisation Christian?

Is an organisation Christian when it has 'Christian values'?

One response to such a question would be that an organisation is Christian because it insists on the primacy of Christian *values* for all its business dealings. Here the assumption is that any organisation is formed by a group of people who voluntarily choose to get together to achieve a shared purpose or task. These people will inevitably be diverse in their worldview and moral structures. There is therefore a need for a common core around which a wide range of people can coalesce.

In such an organisation, the common core is a moral framework of Christian values and there is no need for its members to share the same worldview. If they share certain Christian *values*, it will be possible to ensure that the organisation functions in a way that authentically represents the nature and ministry of Jesus and the values of Scripture.

For example, an organisation might value a basic principle of respect and dignity based on the theological concept of the *imago dei* – that is, individuals have value because everyone reflects something of God. Or, we might state that the work of an organisation should be incarnational – that is, reflecting the fact that Jesus is the Son of God who became a human being and revealed what God is like (John 1:14, 14:7). In the same way, Christians can reveal what Jesus is like.

In this way, the particularities of the Christian faith are distilled into a set of moral values that everyone can adhere to irrespective of faith, colour, creed or culture. An organisation is therefore deemed to be Christian because everyone within it, to varying degrees, acts according to a set of Christian values.

Do Christian values work to keep an organisation faithful?

There are advantages to a values approach. In fact, it is normal for organisations to have values. For example,

- Google has 10 core values emphasising putting the user first and 'Great isn't just good enough.'[1]

- Apple has a creed that begins: 'We believe that we're on the face of the earth to make great products … We're constantly focusing on innovating. We believe in the simple, not the complex.'[2]

- British Petroleum emphasises safety and an excellence that results from a systematic and disciplined approach rather than creative and adventurous flair.[3]

_____

1 See 'Ten things we know to be true', Google, n.d., https://about.google/philosophy/, accessed 22 July 2022.
2 Tim Cook, Apple's current CEO, quoted in Patrick Hull, 'Be Visionary. Think Big.', *Forbes*, 19 December 2012, https://www.forbes.com/sites/patrickhull/2012/12/19/be-visionary-think-big/?sh=3f3cfaf83c17, accessed 27 July 2022.
3 British Petroleum, 'Our Code Our responsibility', bp.com, n.d., https://www.bp.com/

- The Commonwealth Bank of Australia's stated values include doing what is right, getting things done and being accountable.[4]

For a Christian organisation to say that it is based on Christian values is therefore not exceptional in the marketplace, nor is it out of line with common management theory and practice. The Christian values approach is helpful insofar as it provides a common goal and a shared set of guiding values for the moral guidance of an organisation. It would be recognised as a good thing to encourage people to have values such as respect, dignity and worth. To strive to be Christ-like in values and deeds is clearly a worthy goal and does offer a degree of coherence and direction. There are therefore practical advantages to this way of thinking about what makes an organisation Christian.

However, there is a significant theological problem with such an approach to defining the 'Christian-ness' of an organisation. If it were possible to extrapolate values from the Bible and apply them across a broad range of people with varying values and beliefs who can then act Christianly in a way that makes the organisation worthy of the name 'Christian', then there is no real need for Jesus.

If Christianity – following Jesus – is said to be primarily a moral framework marked by the enactment of particular values and actions that anyone can successfully engage with, there is no real need for God other than as the author of the rules that guide the moral practices of the organisation.

The danger here is that we end up with a slightly modified version of deism: a belief that God sets the world in motion, lays down the laws of nature

---

content/dam/bp/business-sites/en/global/corporate/pdfs/who-we-are/our-code-our-responsibility.pdf, accessed 12 September 2022.
4 Commonwealth Bank, 'Our Values', commbank.com.au, n.d., https://www.commbank.com.au/about-us/careers/working-with-us.html#:~:text=Our%20Values,-We're%20a&text=We%20care%20about%20our%20customers,together%20to%20get%20things%20done, accessed 12 September 2022.

(and the moral structures that guide our consciences) and then leaves human beings to do the rest. Within this way of framing the issues, any decent person can adhere to the values and principles of Christianity.

However, Jesus is not a system of moral rules and values. Rather, he is a person. Representing and relating to a person is quite different from representing or relating to a principle or a value. Rules and values may ensure that God is to an extent glorified by the overall moral approach of the organisation, but that does not make the organisation in and of itself Christian. Rules and values may be necessary, but they are clearly not sufficient.

What about a signed Statement of Faith?

In his book *Bullies and Saints: An Honest Look at the Good and Evil of Christian History*, Dr John Dickson, a historian, writer and speaker, offers a series of case studies of the good and evil that Christian believers have done over the centuries. He also contributed the following examples in a personal email.

> Many Christian leaders through history have affirmed and preserved orthodox Christian belief and yet behaved or pursued policies that defy the moral logic of Jesus Christ himself:
>
> - Bishop Ambrose of Milan in the late 4th century was a champion of the Nicene Creed and popular defender of the poor. Yet, he also approved of the Christian destruction of synagogues and refused the emperor's pleas to reimburse the Jewish community.
>
> - Peter 'the Lector' read the Scriptures each Sunday in the 5th-century Alexandrian church. He also led the riot that murdered Hypatia, the most famous (female) philosopher in the city.

- Charlemagne sponsored an educational renaissance in the churches and monasteries of 8th-century Europe. He also conquered the Saxons for the cause of Christ, demanding they choose between 'baptism or the sword' in what scholars have described as a 'Christian jihad'.

- The great 16th-century reformer Martin Luther recovered the Church's dependence upon God's pure grace. Yet his 1543 book *The Jews and the Lies* explicitly called on authorities to 'set fire to Jewish schools and synagogues' and 'confiscate their silver and gold.'[5]

These are just four examples of Christian believers in history behaving in ways that are at odds with the words and deeds of their Saviour.

Fast forward to the last two centuries, and every Christian denomination has witnessed the horrors and shame of members and leaders behaving badly. Some Christian leaders have found to be perpetrators of unspeakable crimes, while others have knowingly covered up the criminal acts of others. Priests, Sunday school teachers and Christian camp directors have gone to jail for paedophilia, and bishops have been stripped of their holy orders.

Soon after his death in 2020, Ravi Zacharias, the founder of a widely respected international evangelical ministry, was found to be not only guilty of many years of serious sexual misconduct but of actively covering them up in a most aggressive way.

In 2021, the Christianity Today podcast series *The Rise and Fall of Mars Hill* chronicled in excruciating detail the bullying and ungodly behaviours of the leadership of the Seattle-based megachurch Mars Hill, which grew from a home Bible study to multiple locations with an average weekly attendance of over 12,000 and then collapsed almost overnight. Podcast host, Mike Cosper,

---

5 John Dickson, email to Stephen Judd, 4 December 2021.

reflected on Mars Hill's demonstrable culture of anger, intimidation and aggression, its 'mob-like and cult-like' following of a narcissistic senior pastor and wondered: 'What was the 'Good News' here? … How did it shape the way the people at the church see Jesus?'[6]

What have Charlemagne, Ravi Zacharias and Mars Hill got to do with our conversation in this book? The answer is that all of these Christian leaders – believers scattered throughout the past two millennia – could fervently assent to the Apostles' Creed, Nicene Creed and any other orthodox statement of faith. Like so many other Christians, they could say that they believed the truths that are in the creeds. But like us all, their actions and behaviour – exhibited in either one or more episodes, or more systemically – were completely ungodly and at odds with the mind of Christ.

Affirmations of faith are clearly no guarantee of godly character or behaviour, and if we think that the ongoing character of Christian organisations can be protected by board and executive members affirming a Statement of Faith, we either are conceited or deluded. Rather, we have to articulate how these Christian truths find expressions in the outlook, disposition, behaviours and daily practices of the organisation. We will turn to this in chapter two.

Review questions

1. Do you think that an organisation can be both Christian and an effective business? If it is not possible, why not?

2. Do you think that it is enough for an organisation to have Christian 'values'? What are the advantages to this approach?

---

6 Mike Cosper (host), 'Aftermath' [podcast], *The Rise and Fall of Mars Hill*, ep. 12, Christianity Today, 4 December 2021.

2. What is organisational faithfulness?

Defining a Christian organisation beyond values or a statement of faith

What we need is a way of respecting the need for rules and values, but at the same time placing them within a broader framework of corporate formation that more closely reflects the nature and purposes of the God who inspires and guides the organisation. In this chapter we will look at the concept of organisational faithfulness.

We would suggest that the gauge for what makes an organisation function in a Christian manner is best found in the idea of *faithfulness*. The writer to the Hebrews describes faith as: 'confidence in what we hope for and assurance about what we do not see' (Heb 11:1). Faithfulness relates to both trust and loyalty: Christians trust in the hope of the gospel even when that hope cannot immediately be seen, and Christians are loyal to God in all things – including our business transactions. Or at least they should be!

When we reflect on the passages from the Gospels we highlighted at the beginning of the previous chapter, the various stories and parables that focused on business had one thing in common: *the outcome of our business practices are gauged by our faithfulness to the mission of the God who gifts, inspires and guides them*. And note that it is God's mission, not ours.

What makes an organisation Christian is not simply the values that it claims to hold (important as such values may well be), but the *way* in which it lives out the vision that it has been given. The Christian-ness of an organisation emerges not simply from shared values, but from the ways in which its Christian-ness creates and inhabits its structures of organisation, management, business practices and relationships. The faithfulness of an organisation emerges from the systematic theological and practical coherence of its various business practices and their relationships to the underlying vision that underpins the organisation as a whole (its faith statements with 'faith' defined as per the definition given to us in Hebrews). The key is not simply values (although it is that), but *faithful participation* in living out those values.

We therefore have an important and potentially creative tension. On the one hand, being a Christian is a personal rather than an organisational experience, requiring a certain set of commitments to Jesus. On the other hand, we recognise that God's kingdom has arrived, albeit partially, and that earthly institutions and organisations have a role to play in participating in God's redemption of the world, even if they are not comprised solely of Christians. Those organisations can be referred to as Christian to the extent that their work participates faithfully in what God is doing. There is tension between our personal faith and our role in Christian organisations living out God's mission on earth. However, resolving this tension could potentially lead to new and creative expressions of mission, as well as leading to deep personal spiritual growth.

Recognising that organisations can participate faithfully in what God is doing means putting God's will into practice in the here and now, 'on earth as it is in heaven' (Matt 6:10). It means ensuring your organisation welcomes in a physical as well as a spiritual reality in which forgiveness and justice reign; a place where the hungry are fed, the orphaned and the widowed and the weak are cared for, the lonely are placed in families, and the sick are healed. Ensuring such faithfulness requires organisation, but it requires organisation of a certain type, what we will call *organisational faithfulness*.

What is organisational faithfulness?

Organisational faithfulness is concerned with the ways in which an organisation participates in God's ongoing mission. It relates to how things are structured and organised, and the general orientation of strategy and management of employees towards the goals of creating life-bringing business enterprises. At its heart, it

- recognises the core identity of an organisation as Christian (seeking to mirror and follow Jesus)
- points towards the type of impact that the organisation desires to have, both internally (with its employees) and externally (towards its clients/ customers, and society more generally).

On the latter point, a faithful organisation makes a significant contribution to the spiritual capital of a society. Spiritual capital relates to the development of models of human authenticity that enrich society, as well as the organisations and communities within that society. Spiritual capital is one way of living out the virtues in public life. It is a way of reclaiming the moral life as publicly significant. Hence, virtues such as patience, self-discipline, gratitude, courage, perseverance, humility and wisdom are put forward and lived out as the basis for a society that is trustworthy.

Spiritual capital sits alongside and complements 'social capital', which draws on the language of economics to describe the intangible wealth that a society shares – for example, historical alliances, values such as hospitality, and norms such as the provision of good-quality educational services.

The three components of organisational faithfulness

Organisational faithfulness has three components:

- ethos, or spirit
- identity
- impact, or outcome.

These components are closely interlinked and co-dependent, as shown below in Figure 1.

Ethos/spirit
Related to the characteristic spirit of the organisation. Its culture and relationships, values and aspirations.

Identity
The intentions and goals of the organisation. Its purpose and mission.

Organisational faithfulness

Impact/ outcome
The effect that an organisation has internally and externally. Its spiritual as well as financial impact.

Figure 1: The three components of organisational faithfulness

The *ethos* is the characteristic spirit of an organisation that is manifested in its culture, relationships, values, and attitudes and aspirations. Christian values contribute to this ethos, but they must be situated within a structure that is Christ-centred. The ethos of the organisation forms the core relational, ethical and spiritual perception of itself.

This ethos emerges from and leads into a specific sense of *identity*, which provides the organisation with its intentions and goals, as well as appropriate ways in which such goals can and should be achieved. In this way, organisations can be underpinned and empowered by the Holy Spirit while at the same time nurturing a Christian spirit – that is, a way of viewing the world that inspires or gives breath to the activities within the organisation.

While recognising that the work of the Holy Spirit is something that God does directly (an act of special or personal grace), nurturing a Christian spirit is a task that everyone can participate in (acts of common grace). In this way, people are shaped, changed and transformed by both the Holy Spirit and Christian spirit.

The third dimension of organisational faithfulness is the *impact* that the organisation has on those whom it seeks to reach. This aspect, once again, has an internal and an external dimension. Internally, the impact is gauged and judged by the organisation's faithfulness to the tasks that have been given to it, alongside of the nature of spiritual development that is experienced by Christians and non-Christians alike within the workplace. Externally, impact is gauged not only by financial loss and gain, but by the types of changes the output of the business encourages. In other words, its success and impact are gauged by spiritual as well as financial capital.

Let us illustrate with a couple of examples.

The fashion label entrepreneur

A fashion label run by a Christian entrepreneur positioned itself as a 'profit with purpose' organisation, donating a percentage of profits to fund an orphanage in Africa. In this way, the organisation's Christian good was entirely linked to its *impact*.

During a Christian program designed to help start-ups innovate and grow, the business team was challenged about the intended supply chain: How would the clothes be manufactured? Were the manufacturing companies paying their employees a livable wage? Where would the material be sourced from? Would the material be using dyes that impacted on the environment?

These questions went to the heart of the *ethos* and *identity* of the organisation. While the business impact was good, its practices would have contributed to the worst elements of the fashion industry. After prayer and reflection, the business team decided to morph the organisation into an online ethical fashion hub. Their Christian vision was to be a leader in setting a new ethical standard in the fashion industry by making it easier for consumers to access ethical fashion.

The Christian aid organisation

Christian development organisations increasingly compete for donor dollars. However, one Christian charity opened itself to challenge over the degree to which it fundraises using 'worldly' techniques at the cost of biblical principles.

For example, does it use the stories of charity partners to guilt donors, thereby stereotyping those partners and evaluating them in terms of their 'compassion value'? This seems to not treat partners as if they are made in the image of God (Gen 1:26–28), or of equal value (Gal 3:28).

Further, did it 'reward' donors, honouring them according to the size of their gifting? This might seem at odds with the apostle James' instruction not to show favouritism (Jas 2:1–4).

This is an issue of *ethos* – that is, the practices they use. However, there was a more fundamental issue of *identity*. The charity had two arms: one with an openly Christian focus, and the other much vaguer about its Christian purpose and denominational connections. The latter was essential for attracting government funding and corporate donations. However, it came with a cost to both to the organisation's integrity and its kingdom *impact*, since some funding precluded them from being open about their Christian *identity* and *ethos*.

The charity has now taken steps to be much clearer about their *identity* and *ethos*, but they have gone one step further with their approach to *impact*. They are trialling a new approach to all donors and partners in the majority world that focuses on developing genuine long-term relationships rather than what have typically been superficial and transactional exchanges.

The significance of founding traditions, deeds and documents

Organisations must constantly be aware of and able to monitor the faithfulness of their Christian ethos. This is done by regularly returning to the foundational traditions, deeds, documents and vision statements and asking the following questions:

- Is the organisation being faithful to the calling that it has been given?
- If not, what changes need to be made?

Reflecting on the foundational traditions, documents and vision statements helps leaders discern where and when even small changes have taken the organisation to the wrong place or headed it in the wrong direction. Such discernment is an opportunity for creative change that ensures the organisation produces an excellent product *and* nurtures and remains faithful to its spirit and its vision.

It is worth noting that foundational motivations and the traditions and practices that derived from them are as important as documented mission and vision statements, which are a comparatively recent phenomenon. Most, if not all, founders of organisations that identify as Christian were very much 'do-ers' of the word (see Jas 1:22), so their vision will be seen in actions and deeds rather than documents. Moreover, many such founders lived at a time when doing God's will and participating in God's redemption of the world was, to them and those around them, simply obvious. It was a command that did not require documentation, and they did not workshop vision statements.

In Western culture and perhaps particularly in business, traditions are too often derided and discarded in favour of the new and innovative. This is understandable, as businesses compete in ever-changing markets and react to ever-changing needs. They need to respond to survive and flourish, and they need to meet the needs and demands of today and tomorrow, not yesterday. Christian organisations are no different. Rather, they need to be countercultural in not discarding those founding visions but rather esteeming them and applying them to the needs, markets and competitive environments in which they find themselves.

There is nothing outmoded in this approach. Rather, it is reflective of the very countercultural characteristics of Christianity itself, which at once treasures the teaching and learnings of the past while at the same time looking enthusiastically to the future. Organisations therefore need to see these founding visions, however expressed – in deeds, documents or traditions – as guides for practice. Such an approach enables an organisation to keep a check on its faithfulness.

Doing an audit of organisational faithfulness

Whether you have a long history as a Christian organisation, or you are a Christian owner of an organisation, or you are a Christian seeking to influence an organisation, it is valuable to engage in an ethos audit that asks these questions:

- Where do we see the organisation's vision working itself out?
- Where do we not see the organisation's vision?
- What needs to be done to ensure that it is seen everywhere?

- What of the organisation's vision is it possible to affirm as a Christian?
- Where does the organisation's vision align with God's mission of making disciples, bringing *shalom* (peace, flourishing, wholeness) and/ or glorifying God?

In this way, an organisation can monitor and reflect on its ethos and in so doing open up the possibility of creative change and faithful practice.

It is important to note that organisational faithfulness is a thoroughly theological endeavour. By this we mean that it is an intellectual and practical expression of what we believe about God. Sometimes we think that theology is purely an intellectual endeavour that is carried out by scholars somewhere far away in the land of the academy! It is obviously important to know what we believe and why we believe it. However, it is equally as important to know what it looks like and feels like to know God.

Knowing God is a subtle mixture of knowing things about God and knowing God. The apostle James tells us that even the demons know more about God than we do. But knowing God is something we do with our bodies as well as our minds. Fundamental to the concept of organisational faithfulness is that faith is a lived entity; it is not simply 'belief'. And that is why faithful Christian expression is to care for the orphans and widows (Jas 1:27) as much as believing with our minds (Matt 22:37). We will look at this more closely in chapter 3.

Review questions

1. If being Christian means to follow Jesus, in what ways does 'organisational faithfulness' imply following Jesus?

2. What do you think of the concept that an organisation is 'Christian' by the faithfulness to the mission of the God who gifts, inspires and guides our practices?

3. Do you think that there is a difference between God's mission and an organisation's mission?

4. Organisational faithfulness has the components of ethos, identity and impact. How are these components expressed in an organisation you might know?

3. In the marketplace, everyone is a theologian

'Well, Peter is no theologian.'[1] We had been invited to a meeting to give feedback on the proposed appointment of a senior executive to a large Christian welfare organisation. All the members of the selection committee were professing Christians. An extensive search had been done by a reputable executive search firm. As far as we could gather, the process had been professional, and the preferred candidate clearly had the skills and experience for the job. Except for one thing: any enquiry into the candidate's belief in Jesus and his depth of biblical knowledge was perfunctory to say the least. All they could say was 'he's no theologian.'

This was an interesting statement. At one level we assumed that they meant the candidate was not an academic biblical scholar and had no formal theological training. Neither of these things were prerequisites for the role. However, at another level perhaps what they meant was that this person had been selected on the basis of his business acumen. The applicant's apparently weak knowledge of and commitment to Jesus seemed to play a secondary role, if in fact it played a role at all.

The idea that someone is 'no theologian' is troublesome, since all Christians are by definition theologians. As soon as you begin to ask questions of who God is, what God does in the world and how that affects your own actions, you are doing theology. R.C. Sproul is dismissive of those who say, 'I don't need theology; I just need to know Jesus.' Although we all need to know Jesus,

---

1 'Peter' is a pseudonym.

we also need to know things about Jesus if we are to know him in any kind of meaningful or transformative sense:

> theology is unavoidable for every Christian. It is our attempt to understand the truth that God has revealed to us – something every Christian does. So it is not a question of whether we are going to engage in theology; it is a question of whether our theology is sound or unsound.[2]

The renowned English academic C.S. Lewis is even more blunt: 'Theology is practical ... if you do not listen to Theology, that will not mean that you have no ideas about God. It will mean that you have a lot of wrong ones.'[3]

Lewis compares theology to a map. You can experience an ocean from the beach and be excited and energised by it. In fact, 'as long as you are content with walks on the beach, your own glimpses are far more fun than looking at a map.' But you need a map if you want to go anywhere on the ocean.[4]

Along similar lines, the apostle Paul urges believers to increase their knowledge of God – to be theologians – so that they are not 'tossed back and forth by the waves, and blown here and there' by the latest fad or by their own ignorance (Eph 4:14). Paul also prays for his own people, who 'are zealous for God, but their zeal is not based on knowledge' (Rom 10:2). In his letter to his colleague Timothy, he emphasises how important it is for us to increase our knowledge of God through Scripture, as it is profitable for 'training in righteousness, so that the servant of God may be thoroughly equipped for every good work' (2 Tim 3:16b–17).

Theology is therefore a prerequisite as Christians go about our daily lives. It is a knowledge base that allows us to operate in the 'real world' maturely, following God's ways rather than misguided worldly wisdom. The statement

---

2 Sproul, *Everyone's a Theologian*, p. 12.
3 Lewis, *Mere Christianity*, p. 155.
4 Ibid., p. 154.

'Well, he's no theologian' is tantamount to saying that he has no idea about God but that that doesn't necessarily matter, as long as his business credentials enable him do the job the organisation has hired him to do. The inference is that the decision-making framework was entirely secular, but that it didn't really matter.

To the contrary, it matters very much.

Why theology matters for Christian organisations

Theology matters because it affects the ways in which an organisation that claims to be Christian operates. Take, for example, the basic narrative that comes to us in Scripture. The Christian believes in a God

- who is the Creator – an eternal, immaterial Mind; the *Logos*, who has created all things
- who has revealed himself to us through Jesus Christ; whose purpose is to reconcile a broken world with its Creator
- whose triune character – Father, Son and Holy Spirit – shows that he is a God of relationships; a God who wants to show God's love to God's creation
- who exhibits grace – a gift freely given to all – enabled through the life, death and resurrection of Jesus
- whose judgement is married to mercy and redemption.

We are creatures who live in a world that has been gifted to us to care for and tend (Gen 1:26–28, 2:15). Part of our caring for this world relates to carefully and creatively looking after God's creation. We don't do this alone, of course. The Holy Spirit gives us guidance and direction, but we are called to participate in what God is doing in the world. Part of that participation is purposefully using the gifts we have been given. This narrative leads to a quite different ethos that includes, but significantly changes, standard business practices. Within this framework, it is hard to imagine an organisation that claims to be Christian being led by people who didn't know or didn't care deeply about such a story.

The appreciation that 'everyone is a theologian' matters for all Christians in all workplaces, not just within organisations that are described as Christian. A person's vocation – their calling from God – can be to many different places, some of which may be overtly Christian and others which are not. No matter where a Christian is placed, they should faithfully approach their work with an enthusiasm and energy that assume the Lord Jesus is sovereign over every organisation. Within this context, they need to be ready to share their faith gently and respectfully with anyone who asks (1 Pet 3:15).

However, the application of our personal and corporate theology matters in a more overt way when Christians are working within those organisations that have been established by Christian individuals, or organisations which make overtly Christian claims: churches, Christian schools, universities, hospitals, aged care and social welfare services, overseas aid and development agencies, business-as-mission entities, and so forth. This is because the foundational motivation of such organisations is inextricably tied to their Christian identity; and in order to nurture and sustain the Christian identity, employees and leaders of organisations need to be able to reflect on their work theologically.

Resolving the tension between individual belief and collective action

In chapter 1, we noted that being a Christian involves personal discipleship – that is, to be a Christian is to follow Jesus. We also discussed how organisations have a role to play in God's redemption of the world. However, that then presents a problem. If 'everyone is a theologian', those within the organisation might be engaged in collective activity, but there is not one understanding or knowledge of God – that is, one theology upon which to base that collective action. Instead, there might be as many understandings, or theologies, as there are individuals involved. There might be different views about

- the nature or character of God
- how that God's character is revealed in the world
- how God's character is reflected in corporate behaviour, if it is reflected at all
- what God's mission is, and how people are called within the organisation to participate in it.

Do you see the problem? It is like a sporting team in which players work hard at their individual skills but each player has their own idea about the purpose and objects of the game and how it should be played.

Church attendance

Some Christian organisations try to resolve this issue by getting board members or executives to affirm that they attend a church. However, this tick-a-box approach not only encourages nominalism, or even disingenuity, but it is also ineffectual. The reasons people go to church are many and varied. Sociologists see two ways that people embed religion into their lives:

- Extrinsic religion: a religion that people hold lightly. They may believe in God, attend church services and even be very involved with the church, but at the end of the day, their religious belief doesn't have much of an impact on their life.
- Intrinsic faith: a personal faith in Jesus and an ability to declare him as Lord which shapes how they see the world and their role in it.

An organisation's requirement to attend church does not distinguish between those with an intrinsic or extrinsic disposition, let alone discern those who overstate their enthusiasm for sitting in the pews.

Statement of Faith

Another attempt at solving this problem is by settling upon a simple Statement of Faith. This might incorporate one or more of the Christian creeds – for example, the Apostles' and the Nicene Creeds.

While this has been a long-term practice, we no longer believe it is adequate. Increasingly, the words of the creeds are understood in very different ways by those who profess to be Christians. For example, there are bishops within the Anglican Communion who regard evangelicals who believe in the authority of the Bible as somewhat quaint; there are Catholics whose worldview is seen through the lens of a common grace rather than a personal saving grace; there are Southern Baptists whose worldview is very different to Presbyterians, and so on. Further, as was demonstrated earlier, an affirmation of belief is no guarantee of godly behaviour.

So, what is the solution? How do we resolve the dissonance between individual belief and collective action? How can we have clarity about what the organisation's understanding and knowledge of God is?

A Statement of Organisational Theology

We believe that what is needed is a detailed Statement of Organisational Theology. Such a statement will take our knowledge of God and articulate how it applies in every activity of an organisation, be it a school, overseas aid agency, pension fund, welfare organisation, health and aged care service, or whatever endeavour that Christian organisation is engaged in.

What we mean by a Statement of Organisational Theology is a statement which *articulates the ethos of the organisation*, as we discussed in chapter one. It is a statement that

- undergirds how an organisation's policies on human resources, finance, risk or strategy are developed
- is reflected in the organisation's policies and processes, and even more importantly, its behaviour
- takes the knowledge of God and articulates how that is applied every activity of the organisation
- is frequently referred to, facilitates a continuous ethos audit, and helps to shine a light on the faithfulness of the organisation.

What should be in such a Statement of Organisational Theology? That is for each organisation to decide for itself. The statement of a Christian school will look different to that of a pension fund; that of a hospital different to that of an overseas aid agency. However, in the following chapters we look at 12 core elements that we think trustees, board members and leaders would do well to consider including in their own Statement of Organisational Theology.

Review questions

1. What do you think about the idea that 'everyone is a theologian'? What difference does it make to how you view your everyday life?

2. Does it matter that 'everyone is a theologian' when Christians act collectively? What could be some of the strengths and weaknesses?

3. Kevin Vanhoozer says that 'theological competence is ultimately a matter of being able to make judgements that display the mind of Christ.'[5] What do you think of this statement? Does it impact on your decision-making?

---

5 Vanhoozer, *The Drama of Doctrine*, p. 2.

4. Have you experienced any circumstances where the faith of individual Christians is not found expression in the actions of the Christian organisation? What do you think can be done about that?

5. How might the concept of a Statement of Organisational Theology bridge the gap between individual faith and collective practice in your organisation?

Towards a Theology for Organisations

We have established that Christian organisations, and Christians influencing organisations, are tested by their faithfulness to God's mission. Measures of faithfulness include ethos (its culture and spirit), its Christian identity, and the kingdom impact of the organisation.

In discussing the failure of faith and values statements to provide assurances that a Christian organisation will retain their Christian identity and/ or be Christian in their practices, we talked about the need for organisations to develop a theological statement that governs behaviour.

In the next two sections we will look at key elements that might shape such an organisational theology statement. This section covers eight foundational elements: sin, judgement, grace, faith, hope, trust, forgiveness and redemption.

4. Why your organisation might be sinful without you even noticing it

There are many ways in which we could start to develop an organisational theology. We might think that 'obviously' we begin with grace or forgiveness or love. Clearly these theological concepts are important. However, we would like to begin from a slightly different perspective, the perspective of sin. We begin here because there is something very important that needs to be pointed out at the start.

Let us begin by thinking a little differently about sin. When we think of sin, we usually think about things we might have done wrong. 'I shouldn't have told that lie.' 'I shouldn't have had that thought.' 'I shouldn't have been thinking about my lunch during the sermon.' However, sin is much more complicated than what we should or shouldn't have done.

In the first seven chapters of the book of Romans, the apostle Paul writes about sin and evil. He describes how humans were handed over by God to a 'depraved mind, so that they do what ought not to be done', because they did not 'think it worthwhile to retain the knowledge of God' (Rom 1:28–30). Evil, Paul says, is found in the things that people do when they substitute themselves and their perspective for God. The primary problem for human beings lies in their failure to 'acknowledge God, name God as God, and accept that God cannot be reduced to the self.'[1]

---

[1] Eastman, 'The "Empire of Illusion"', p. 5.

An 'Empire of Illusion'

If we substitute ourselves for God, then we end up with a false picture of the world. If we cannot see the world clearly, we cannot live and act faithfully within it. We end up living in what Chris Hedges has called an 'Empire of Illusion.'[2] It is impossible to escape from the Empire of Illusion, because by definition it is illusory; we can't see it. Think for a moment about the killing of George Floyd. Onlookers were horrified by what they saw, as were the millions of people who watched it on television.[3] Yet the policemen involved seemed to see nothing wrong in their actions. They had been trained to see the world in quite a different way from others. They were involved in sinful actions but didn't notice their sin. When evil becomes invisible, it is impossible to resist.

Later in Romans, Paul talks about sin as a form of power – a power that is impossible to overcome without the grace of God (Rom 3:9, cf. 5:6). Further, we believe it is a power that embeds itself not only in individuals, but within systems (as suggested in Romans 5:12–13). One of the conclusions of this book is that organisations cannot be Christian. Only people can come to know Jesus, repent and be saved. As we have already mentioned, organisations have a spirit – an ethos – that underpins the way they structure themselves. And that spirit is not necessarily a force for good.

You may not have thought about it, but organisations (including churches!) can suffer from poor mental health – even psychosis. If you are on the inside, everything may feel normal, but anyone looking in can see that things are a mess. Or the organisation may be depressed, and everyone working there is flat, disheartened, unenthusiastic, lost. Organisations can also become neurotic, anxious, distracted – the list goes on.

---

2 Hedges, *Empire of Illusion*.

3 See, for example, 'George Floyd: What happened in the final moments of his life', *BBC News*, 16 July 2020, https://www.bbc.com/news/world-us-canada-52861726, accessed 3 August 2022.

Organisations can also become pathogenic and sinful: filled with the wrong kind of spirit. This is at least part of what Paul is referring to when he talks about the authorities and powers in Ephesians 6:12: 'For our struggle is not against flesh and blood, but against the rulers, against the authorities, against the powers of this dark world and against the spiritual forces of evil in the heavenly realms.' Pathogenic systems become agents of the power of sin: the conduits through which sin manifests itself.

The power of sin

The crucial point here is that you do not have to intend to be sinful to carry out sin. You just need to lose your sense of truth versus falsehood and allow yourself to become cognitively dislocated and disoriented from the fundamental reality that is God. When we start to talk about the only truth being *my* truth, or that truth is flexible and 'Anyway, who knows what is true?', we take the first steps towards being drawn away from the truth that is God and towards the power that is sin.

Thus, evil and sin manifest themselves when we fail to see God, mistake ourselves for God and just walk off in the wrong direction. God lets us do that. His response (wrath) is not fire from heaven, but rather simply allowing people to yield to their own desires.

The point here is important: you can think you have a good and successful organisation that is functioning well according to the criteria you set down, but that apparent success may be an illusion. You can look at your organisation and say 'Yes! This is great', but when God looks at it what does he see? It is crucial that we are aware that what we think we see may be illusory.

Employing lukewarm Christians with untransformed minds may lead to the success of an organisation, but you may well lose its soul. Only when our minds are transformed can we see God clearly, which is why acknowledging our sin is a wise place to begin our reflections on organisational theology.

Honouring God is not optional for your 'Christian' organisation

In Exodus 20:7, we find the third commandment: 'You shall not misuse the name of the LORD your God.' You might ask the question, 'What's swearing got to do with Christian organisations and organisational theology?'

Well, there is a little more going on in the third commandment than simply swearing or making oaths. Elsewhere in the Bible, it is clear that God doesn't take kindly to people misusing his name (Ezek 20:9). He puts a high value on his name and values his reputation. He is deeply saddened, even angered, when things are done in his name that are unworthy. Just as we don't like being verballed, God doesn't like it either.

That should give those in organisations that are called 'Christian' a reason to pause, think hard and even fearfully reflect about how their conduct and the corporate conduct of the organisation gives glory to God or, alternatively, whether they profane God's name 'in the eyes of the nations among whom they lived' (Ezek 20:9). Do they reflect God's character in everything that they do? In their strategy? In their human resources management, which is just business speak for how you relate and interact with staff members? In how they use their finances? In how they interact with their clients, students, patients, funders or regulators?

Christian organisations need to ensure that their actions carried out in God's name actually honour God. And one way of doing this is to have a vibrant, living, well-articulated organisational theology. Otherwise, either by commission or omission, by premediated intent or by ignorance, we misuse God's name and offend him. And that is a position that we should fearfully avoid.

Review questions

1. Chris Hedges points to the way in which sin can be problematic because is often difficult to see. Why is this important for Christian organisations?

2. If organisations can be sinful in this way, how might they counter that?

3. In Romans 12:2, Paul says 'Do not conform to the pattern of this world, but be transformed by the renewing of your mind.' How might this be applied to organisations?

4. Do you think that the third commandment, 'You shall not misuse the name of the Lord your God' has relevance to organisations that identify as Christian and, if so, how?

5. Judgement: you are what you tolerate

This chapter begins with a story.

Chris was a general manager of a large national Christian disability organisation. He reported to the chief executive officer, Mark. Chris was well-connected in the sector and had grown his division significantly from the ground up. Its innovative services gained national recognition.

The problem was that Chris saw the division as 'his' division. He didn't like 'his' people working with other parts of the company or others putting their nose into his 'patch'.

One day CEO Mark organised an operational workshop and asked Cheryl, one of the local managers who reported to Chris, to present on some issues and innovations in their service. Cheryl put in a lot of effort preparing her presentation and was excited and very nervous. She was proud of what her team had done.

Chris didn't say anything before the meeting, but he was not happy. He might have thought that all of this should have been funnelled through him, and perhaps it could have been. Maybe he thought he should have presented rather than Cheryl.

After Cheryl presented, Chris belittled her in front of the entire room, caustically criticising her presentation. Perhaps in his view he had asserted his authority. However, the rest of the room was stunned into silence and Cheryl, normally robust, was shaken and close to tears.

The next day the CEO had a one-on-one with Chris. Mark told him that such behaviour by a senior executive was unacceptable and that he must apologise to Cheryl and, indeed, should probably apologise to everyone else who had been present.

Chris didn't see it that way. 'Are you trying to get rid of me?' he asked Mark. 'Not at all,' replied Mark. 'But I am calling out your behaviour, which I consider unacceptable.'

The meeting ended shortly afterwards. If Chris apologised to Cheryl, no-one heard about it. He certainly said no more about the matter to the group. Within a matter of weeks Chris resigned, left the company and quickly secured another job.

Chris was a high-performing senior executive. From an operational performance point of view, his departure was a loss to that organisation. However, if he had stayed and there had not been repentance or restoration, the outcome would have been far worse. The clear, non-verbal signal to other staff like Cheryl would have been to keep your head down and don't express your ideas or thoughts freely. Further, other staff would have been nervous about stepping out of line as far as Chris was concerned. From Mark's position, if he had said or done nothing, it would have been tantamount to saying Chris' behaviour was accepted and acceptable. He had to hold Chris accountable for his actions.[1]

While there are many vital elements in a Christian organisational theology, judgement is vital. You cannot behave indifferently or tolerate underperformance or worse. Rather, as a leader and as an organisation the daily mantra should be 'I am what I tolerate. We are what we tolerate.'

---

[1] This case study was previously noted in Judd, Robinson & Errington, *Driven by Purpose*, pp. 185–186.

Judgement can be a costly principle

'You are what you tolerate' can be a costly principle to stand by.

In 2005 a staff member at a nursing home blew the whistle. She alleged that four of her fellow workers had sexually harassed a non-ambulant resident and laughed it off as a bit of a gag.

This was in the days before mandatory reporting of such incidents or allegations to the police. Instead, over the course of two weeks the nursing home manager conducted interviews with seven witnesses as well as the alleged perpetrators, who denied the allegations. The alleged victim was unable to communicate verbally, although other staff noted that his non-verbal communication improved markedly after the four staff members were suspended. At the conclusion of the investigation, the employment of the four staff members was terminated.

In response to their termination, the four staff members took their case to the Industrial Relations Commission. The nursing home provider refused to settle out of court. The case was heard, with the nursing home provider vigorously defending its decision. The Industrial Relations Commissioner found that while the alleged incidents 'probably' happened and the nursing home had reasonable cause to terminate the employees, there had been procedural errors in the internal investigations. After concluding that reinstatement was unworkable, the Commissioner awarded the former employees monetary compensation for their termination of employment.

The CEO of the nursing home communicated to all staff what had occurred, carefully ensuring that they only used the published words in the commissioner's decision. The response from staff was astonishing. The whistleblowers were pleased that their actions had been supported, while other staff now said they felt confident to come forward in a similar situation. Still others were proud that their organisation did not ignore such behaviour.

Should this company have settled out of court? Some would say that this would have been the 'commercial thing to do' or perhaps even the biblical model (Matt 5:25). However, settling, which might have involved reinstatement, would have sent all the wrong signals to the rest of the workforce about what behaviour would be tolerated. It would also have discouraged others from raising concerns while perhaps encouraging others to seek unfair compensation in the sure knowledge that the company had the pockets but not the stomach for the contest.[2]

Judgement might prove costly, but an organisation is what it tolerates.

The organisational terrorist

Leaders and organisations struggle most with the implications of judgement when it involves someone who is highly capable and fairly senior. That person might be clever, passionate, ambitious and technically strong in their field. These qualities are all good things, but they often lead to an inflated self-belief, with the individual convincing others that they are indispensable to the organisation's fortunes. These people are often quite charismatic, and invariably they gather a coterie of followers who are 'their' people.

And that is the make-up of what might be called the 'organisational terrorist'. They will destroy the organisation, cultivate 'palace intrigues', and hoard or control information to make themselves look better or superior in the eyes of the broader group. Because of the damaging effects of their behaviour on an organisation, they must be held to account – no matter how competent they may be.

Consider this example. Dr Smith had a reputation as a good clinician and had significant responsibility within her hospital. While she had a group of loyal supporters, for years she had shown little respect for a number of other

---

2 Case study previously noted in Judd, Robinson & Errington, pp. 186–187.

staff members and the organisation which employed her. She bullied staff, demonstrated contempt for her seniors, and sought to develop a fiefdom within the organisation. Complaints had been made and warnings issued, but her behaviour did not change.

There were all sorts of reasons why nothing had been done: there was a fear that Dr Smith and her acolytes might leave, resulting in a gap in expertise. Complainants were scared to pursue their complaints, while other medical professionals were seemingly reluctant to rock the boat. Whatever the reasons, the behaviour had been tolerated for too long.

Ultimately, there was an incident where Dr Smith bullied and humiliated a junior staff member in front of her peers. The staff member complained to the People and Culture (P&C) team (the human resources department), alleging that had other staff members behaved in that way, they would be disciplined. The junior staff member questioned whether there was one rule for some and another rule for others.

The P&C team raised the complaint with Dr Smith and cited previous warnings about her behaviour. This performance interview was conducted in accordance with protocols and held with a union representative present. Dr Smith pushed back hard and was completely unrepentant. A report was prepared, and as the organisation moved to terminate her contract, Dr Smith recognised that her abilities would be best served in another hospital and quickly departed.

The telling epilogue of this story was that none of the feared outcomes of mass departures or poorer clinical performance occurred. In fact, the team's performance improved, and what one person described as a 'wonderful breeze of fresh air' moved through the entire hospital, not just Dr Smith's department.

The lasting lesson is that you should never walk away from doing the just thing because you are afraid of possible repercussions. You are indeed what you tolerate.

Judgement under pressure

In the previous examples, their context provided space for considered and thoughtful processes. The decisions took time, and while they may or may not have always been right, they were certainly faithful.

There are other times, however, when time is limited and the outcome seems harsh and unforgiving. During the early days of the pandemic in 2020 we know of one hospital where a nurse manager ignored the proper use of personal protective equipment (PPE) and scoffed at others who took PPE use seriously. Their actions, which constituted a knowing and serious breach of infection control protocols, were putting lives at risk. A staff member raised her concerns with management, the matter was investigated and the nurse manager was immediately removed from their position and left the hospital. Was that response too harsh? Some might think so. Sometimes, unfortunately, we do not have the luxury of time. All that we can ask of decision-makers is that they do their utmost to be faithful when holding others accountable.

Exercising judgement in schools

All of us have memories of our time at school. Some memories are happy, while other memories may leave lasting scars. Our experiences at school are formational and some of the memories that scar us involve the exercise of judgement.

Dr Timothy Wright was Headmaster of The Shore School in Sydney, Australia for 17 years until he retired at the end of 2019. Wright describes the tension between justice and love:

> In school discipline there is a constant tension between the demands of mercy and that of justice. The disciplinary philosophy of a Christian School must be grounded in the understanding set out in scripture that discipline is an act of love (Hebrews 12:7–11)

and that the school community must operate with norms established and curated by a Head who understands his/her role as magistrate of that community. It is therefore unwise to set out the policy as a black and white penal code (if person X does Y then automatically Z is the consequence). Every head of school operating in such a way finds themselves carrying out decisions with unintended and unjust consequences (and yes, the author learned this through bitter experience). Codes should be based on principles, not detailed prescriptive codes, and the phrase 'may be the consequence' is powerful when discretion is needed.

However, it is unjust for there to be no consequence and the issue of grace plays a part here. It is not kind nor just for students to threaten the well-being of others, and whether it be bullying, sale of drugs, continual sabotage of the classroom or humiliation of teachers, the school community cannot tolerate such breaches of norms. So the decisions of exclusion or retention are often a balance between the needs of the individual and the needs of the community.[3]

Judgement must be a key component of an organisation's theology. Without it an organisation will be swayed by what is popular, what is contemporary practice, what is commercially viable or what is practically expedient.

Let us now look at another must-have element that should be part of an organisational theology: Grace.

Review questions

1. What do you think of the statement 'you are what you tolerate'?

2. Can you think of examples when bad behaviour or poor performance was tolerated? What was the outcome?

---

[3] Tim Wright, email to Stephen Judd, 21 February 2021.

3. In this chapter there are examples of where judgement as a principle was costly, in both financial and personnel terms? Is the cost always worth it?

4. God's judgement is just. Is judgement justly exercised in organisations you are familiar with? If not, why not and what could be done about it?

5. In this chapter there is reference to 'organisational terrorists', people who are highly competent but do not share the organisation's vision and values, who undermine the ethos or identity of the organisation. Can you think of any examples of such 'terrorists'? How do you think they can be best managed?

6. There is the claim in this chapter that it is not just for there to be no consequences for poor behaviour. Do you agree?

6. Reflecting God's grace

There is no more central concept in Christian theology than grace. Some theologians have even suggested that the very essence of theology is grace.[1] But what do people mean by grace? Not only are there different understandings of the word, but the way it is applied in a Christian organisation will have a significant impact on the organisation itself.

For the purposes of this discussion, we will be using the commonly accepted meaning of grace as *the free gift of reconciliation with God*. It something that humans do not deserve, either collectively or as individuals, and it is not won by merit or earned by work. As the American writer and theologian Frederick Buechner says:

> Grace is something you can never get but can only be given. There's no way to earn it or deserve it or bring it about any more than you can deserve the taste of raspberries and cream or earn good looks or bring about your own birth.[2]

Common grace and special grace

Among Christians there is a shared, acknowledged need for grace, because humankind is out of relationship with its Maker. However, the acknowledgement of the need for grace is often where the agreement among Christians ends.

That is because while some Christians rely on what is called 'common grace', others focus on 'special grace'. While 'special grace' involves the redemption or making right with himself that God gives to the individuals

---

1 Sproul, *Everyone's a Theologian*, p. 215, quoting Berkhouwer.

2 Buechner, *Beyond Words*, p. 139.

who accept Jesus as their Saviour, 'common grace' includes the merciful and kind gifts that God gives to all people, universally. Jesus says that God 'causes his sun to rise on the evil and the good and sends rain on the righteous and the unrighteous' (Matt 5:45). Importantly for our conversation, common grace is seen not just in such natural events, but also in the positive results that accrue to human society through the efforts of those involved in health, aged care, welfare and overseas aid agencies, in schools and other educational institutions, and even government. The common grace of God is seen to be working through the people who endeavour to advance the common good.

While all Christians acknowledge the mercy and kindness of God to all of his creation that is common grace, conservative Protestants are more likely to emphasise the priority of special grace, the free gift of salvation – of restored relationship with God – to those who accept Jesus as their Lord, acknowledge him as their Saviour and seek to be his disciples. By contrast, the understanding of many other Christians is that God's grace is primarily seen as working in the whole of creation.

While this distinction may be lost on the secular world, it has enormous implications for Christian organisations. If your understanding of God's grace is that it is primarily God's goodness and mercy to all of his creation, then that understanding will determine whom you recruit. It means that while the activity of the organisation is important – excellent hospital care, good educational standards, development work in needy nations and so on – you are not particularly concerned whether the recruit is a Christian or not, or what they believe. That is a secondary issue, because God will use them for his purposes, and, of course, that is true. God does use all believers and unbelievers alike to fulfil his purposes (e.g. Naaman in 2 Kings 5 and the Persian kings in the books of Ezra and Nehemiah).

However, the kingdom of God does not become visible through common grace. The kingdom is established through disciples – that is, people who know and understand Jesus and the mission of God in their organisation and who are able to live it out and speak it out. It requires people who can witness to Jesus, however imperfectly, and it requires people who seek to follow the promptings of the Holy Spirit, as much as is possible as sinners.

The appreciation of the distinction between common grace and special grace and its place in shaping how a Christian organisation sees its role in God's redemption of the world is a vital element in an organisational theology.

Grace at work

If God's grace to us is expressed in his mercy and kindness, how do Christian organisations reflect God's grace to others?

Tim Wright offers some answers as to how grace is expressed in a Christian organisation:

> It seems to me that grace is more commonly expressed in organisations by the little things. Or, rather, while they might be little in the overall scheme of the things for the organisation as a whole, they are very significant to the persons who are the recipients. They are personal; they are unearned gifts freely given.
>
> It might be simple 'random' acts of kindness. It might be quietly providing emergency support for a staff member fleeing domestic violence; it might be financially supporting another following the death of a son; or another struggling with addiction. It might be giving another extended leave to look after a sick family member. Clearly it is going beyond what the policies say, without counting the cost.[3]

'Without counting the cost.' We must expect that compassion will come at a cost: financial cost, as well as organisational or personal sacrifice. If we are cost-counters, we may struggle to show compassion and grace. But our

---

[3] Tim Wright, email to Stephen Judd, 21 February 2021.

challenge is to not count the cost – because followers of Jesus don't. God honours compassionate grace.

We know of a Christian employer who supported a worker who suffered from addiction following the tragic death of a child. The employer supported her through her rehab. Years later, the worker is a mentor to many others.

Elsewhere, it might be that the organisation supports someone whose condition is outside its normal remit. In retirement villages, it might be accommodating that person who can't afford the entry contribution; in welfare services, it might be actively engaging with other groups who find jobs for women who have been homeless as a result of domestic violence and who often have a criminal record.

One correspondent told this moving story about a staff member he knew who was bipolar:[4]

> Chee had periods of being 'unwell' and I think he would have been medically 'retired' in some other organisations. On one occasion during my time, Chee came into the office seriously unwell and walking round the office in a state of panic and confusion. I knew that the compassion I was able to extend to him at that time ran across the organisation, so rather than be let go, he was given a seriously long period of time off and one of the General Managers quietly visited him once a month to ensure that the relationship and connectedness did not break down … such actions have an osmotic impact across the organisation.

Chee finally returned to work and years later continues to be one of the most valued employees in that organisation.

These stories show us how God's grace can be reflected in a Christian organisation. While there are many ways this can happen, Tim Wright's observations give us a good place to start:

---

4 Email from anonymous correspondent sent to Stephen Judd in 2021.

- *The behaviour of leaders.* What leaders might think are small actions have big consequences. It is therefore important to express compassion and love to those around us – both employees and those we serve – when they are doing it tough. We have been constantly amazed at the impact that 'simple acts of kindness' have on those who receive it. Long after everyone else has forgotten about it, the recipient of the kindness has an enduring memory of the love and grace that was extended to them.
- *Acting 'beyond what the policies say.'* Too often, organisations slavishly serve their policies rather than having the policies serve them. Shielded by policies, they decline to admit that needy older person to the retirement village; they terminate that good employee who has bipolar disorder; they are inflexible when more leave is required than the computer allows.
- *Acting faithfully and rightly 'without counting the cost.'* God's grace to us through Jesus is a freely given gift. How can an organisation that bears his name then be miserly in response?

Some readers will be severely troubled by this sort of wild talk. The P&C team will be thinking that we have lost the plot in endorsing Wright's cavalier approach to policies; the Finance team will declare it reckless and irresponsible in ignoring the fundamental importance of keeping a vigilant, tight rein on a company's finances. However, we would argue that to give expression to grace within a Christian organisation must invariably be personal, outrageously counter to the rules, as well as costly. It is much like God's grace to us!

Review questions

1. Grace is a gift of God that is not won by merit or earned by work. How do you define or picture grace?
2. In this chapter the differences between common grace and special (or personal) grace are discerned. What are your thoughts on how these forms are grace are expressed in an organisation?

3. How might an emphasis on one rather than the other affect how a Christian organisation functions? How does it impact, including on its recruitment policies?

4. While God uses all people to fulfil his purposes, do you agree that for the kingdom of God to come into sight, God requires disciples who know Jesus and who can witness to him?

5. Can you identify some expressions of God's grace being reflected in actions at an organisation you are familiar with? Do you agree it is in the simple acts? Or in bigger structural things? Or both?

7. Faith, hope and trust

A focus on grace leads us into the important areas of faith, hope and trust, which are the natural response to the one who shows us grace. The writer to the Hebrews describes faith as having 'confidence in what we hope for and assurance about what we do not see' (11:1). In Colossians 1:15, the apostle Paul describes Jesus in this way: 'The Son is the image of the invisible God, the firstborn over all creation.' Both of these passages offer an important perspective in relation to our walk with God. Faith involves putting our *trust* in a God that we cannot see, and having our *hope* held secure in the one who is sovereign over all creation.

This, of course, is completely countercultural. Think about it in this way. Our worldview is shaped by many things such as culture, religion, philosophy and the media. One powerful philosophical belief that shapes our worldview is empiricism. Empiricism is the philosophical argument that only that which falls upon the retina of the eye can be true. In other words, if you can't see it, measure it or touch it, it can't exist. So, if someone asks us to place our trust in a God whom we cannot see, it sounds ridiculous! However, what we need to bear in mind is that empiricism is philosophical belief. There is no empirical evidence for empiricism! You have to put your faith in the philosophy in order to believe it.

Therefore, faith – being sure of what you hope for and certain of what you cannot see – is not something that only Christians live by. Faith is actually a cultural imperative that everyone in the Western world lives by implicitly or explicitly. Faith is the way that we make sense of the world. Without it we have nothing to be sure of and nothing to be certain of. We are limited to what we can see.

As well as functioning as a useful apologetic in response to those who seek to ridicule faith in the name of science and reason, and challenging those who can only see business in terms of physical outcomes, this way of thinking about faith raises the question of how it relates to individuals in organisations. How does faith, and its necessary companions hope and trust, help us to function more faithfully in the workplace?

Precision in policy

Being sure of what you hope for and certain of what you cannot see might sound like an odd basis for business or business-related relationships. However, it does lead to an interesting challenge: do managers trust their staff members? Are they sure of what to hope for from them and are they certain that it will occur when they cannot see them?

In the last few years, many companies have instituted policies on how their staff should personally interact with social media. This is understandable: whereas previously staff members might gossip at the local shops about their employer and their work colleagues, now social media postings have made it possible to broadcast perspectives and views in a much more public way. Many social media policies include precise directives, such as when and where staff can engage in social media, while some even state that online activity after hours which is in breach of the company's code of conduct may subject the staffer to disciplinary action or termination.

The challenge for organisations is that if they want to have internal social media regulations that are characterised by precision, they then inevitably engage in a ceaseless race to update their regulations in order to keep them relevant as new forms of media emerge, and unexpected scenarios occur.

In addition, most of this policy formation and reformation occurs within P&C departments without reference to either effective or ineffective regulation. Researchers Professor John Braithwaite, Toni Makkai and Valerie Braithwaite report that:

> The pursuit of precision, either by protocols or by the proliferation of ever-narrower rules, causes an unreliability that is a symptom of a deeper and many-sided malaise of regulatory failure. This is especially depressing since the pursuit of precision usually fails in its own terms – failure to deliver precision.[1]

Despite such evidence, we acknowledge that some readers will be more comfortable with regularly issuing a new policy or directive whenever a gap is discerned in the organisation's commandments of 'dos and don'ts'.

But let's think about it for a moment. Unless we are in an 18th-century factory overseen by a vigilant command-control superintendent or a modern-day sweatshop, all organisations have to run on trust. The 'boss' cannot be all-overseeing and all-knowing. An overseas aid agency will have workers in distant lands; schoolteachers will be in the classroom without supervision; a home-care worker will be travelling from one client's house to another. And following the COVID-19 pandemic, more people than ever continue working from home, geographically separated from those to whom they reported, leading to an increased need for employers to trust their employees.

Whether employees are in the same room or working remotely, trust is core to effective organisations. It is not blind trust, nor is it naïve. In fact, we need to be realistic that sometimes trust will be misplaced, there will be disappointments and people will let you down. Nor are we promoting some form of libertarian anarchy. Rather, a trusting organisation has an approach of 'freedom within a framework', a series of broad principles of what is the agreed way to behave and work and relate.

---

1 Braithwaite, Braithwaite & Makkai, *Regulating Aged Care*, p. 230.

Freedom within a framework

One of us (Stephen) recalls how he worked with staff when he was a CEO of a major care organisation. Within that context, his attitude towards and relationships with staff was based on the principles of faith, hope and trust. His approach was to trust people until it was demonstrated that such trust was ill-placed. He trusted (that is, had faith in them) that they were transparent with him, would not cover up issues or failings, and would be frank and forthright. When he heard about something that was not right – a complaint, for example – he would have it investigated, with the full knowledge of any staff that were involved in the matter. Similarly, he believed that as staff were trusted with caring for clients in their own homes, the organisation should trust staff members with other administrative matters, such as petty cash. Certainly, there were times when the organisation was disappointed (such as a rare instance of theft from a client), but a presumption that there would be likely wrongdoing, starting from a position in which faith and trust in staff was not assumed, inevitably produced policies, processes and protocols that tied everyone up in knots and reduced employee engagement.

The dress code document

Years ago, a health and aged care organisation decided that a dress code was required for its home care and residential care home staff. The reason was that, in the absence of a uniform that was deemed 'institutional', some staff were dressing in a way that clients and residents felt was disrespectful – for example, wearing clothes that were too casual, too revealing during the act of care or better suited to other contexts.

Much executive effort was put into this dress code document, and precise details went into the document about what was – and was not – acceptable. Trendy ripped shirts, singlets, miniskirts and jeans were out. Further questions were asked and deliberated on. Were crop tops out? Answer: yes. Which body piercings were okay? Answer: well, it depends. If thongs/flip flops are out, what about dress shoes that are not enclosed? Answer: we can't remember the determination. Fashions changed almost as quickly as the document was developed, and a blizzard of questions were asked by local managers anxious to have someone else adjudicate on fashion. More and more protocols and definitions were added to the document.

Tired of it all, the Chief Financial Officer settled the matter. Normally a quiet and understated fellow, one morning he walked into a senior executive meeting in thoroughly inappropriate attire, even though what he wore was precisely compliant with the formal dress code. The point was well-made. From that moment, the policy was discarded. All staff members were reminded of the organisation's overarching statements that affirmed respect for the people they served and with whom they worked. They were reminded that their shared employment framework promised there would be open, honest and timely communication with each other. It was therefore up to the manager, on a case-by-case basis, to have a quiet chat to someone if their dress sense might be inappropriate or offend. It was a management by exception approach, and it was an approach that was also mindful of demographic differences: what was appropriate dress for one 'proper' well-to-do client was different for those staff who worked with homeless clients on the street.

Being trusted begets trust

A 'freedom within a framework' model that is built on faith and trust requires people to respect and value each other within the workplace. In turn, it is far more enduring and all-encompassing – for example, covering all forms of communication, not just social media.

Approaching workplace relationships from the standpoint of mutual trust and faith within the company has huge dividends in terms of employee engagement and a positive workplace culture. Being trusted means that the organisation says to an employee 'You belong; you are worthy of trust.' Also, being trusted begets trust. Where a directive-driven approach is by its very nature untrusting and driven by inferred suspicion, trust empowers employees and leads to higher performance.

We should not be surprised by this. An analogy is how a great football team performs. Regardless of the football code, if you are a player in a great team you are trained to trust the teammate next to you. You rely on them to perform, so you don't leave your position and tackle the player they are marking. They, in turn, know that they are trusted with that 'mark' and will work hard not to let you or the team down. By contrast, we have all seen teams where that mutual trust is absent and for whom winning is a rarity.

Faith, hope and trust are core drivers of operational performance, but they are more than that. Just as they are at the heart of the personal experience of a Christian, faith, hope and trust should also be hallmarks of a Christian organisation. Yes, there will be people who disappoint us, there will be times when we disappoint others, and there will be those who let the organisation down, sometimes grievously. But does that not reflect the Christian experience where we personally 'fall short of the glory of God' (Rom 3:23)? Where we, with almost unerring and shameful regularity, let Jesus down?

The upside – the huge dividend – of an approach that reflects 'the freedom within a framework' reflecting the way God generously treats us, is that the vast majority of an organisation's staffers are affirmed as trusted team members who belong and are valued, whose self-worth and worth to the organisation underpins their job satisfaction, and whose commitment to the organisation is reflected in their performance. It might be an approach that feels countercultural, but it works, and it's an expression of organisational faithfulness in action.

Review questions

1. Can organisations operate on faith, hope and trust? What are the advantages and disadvantages of such an approach? Can you give examples?

2. What do you think of the approach of 'freedom within a framework', a series of broad principles on what is the agreed way to behave and work and relate as a means of developing a trusting organisation?

3. Why is trust so important to employee engagement?

4. Sometimes we are let down by people in whom we had trust. In such situations, our faith will be tested. What should be our response?

8. Experiencing forgiveness in the workplace

'Forgive us our sins, for we also forgive everyone who sins against us' (Luke 11:4).

Christians and non-Christians alike would be familiar with these words from the Lord's Prayer, the prayer that Jesus taught his disciples. This is because a core tenet of Christianity is forgiveness for 'sins', which damage our relationship with God and with each other.

The apostle John instructs us that 'if anybody does sin, we have an advocate with the Father – Jesus Christ, the Righteous One. He is the atoning sacrifice for our sins, and not only for ours but also for the sins of the whole world' (1 John 2:1–2).

However, within some organisations there does not appear to be a lot of forgiveness. It might be the case that Christians within these organisations – and the policies of the organisations – emphasise how forgiveness applies to their personal relationship to God rather than how they treat those around them. There seems to be a group forgetfulness of the second part of the prayer: 'as we forgive those who sin against us.'

Over the course of decades of professional life, we have witnessed too often Christian organisations resorting to 'performance management' and 'final warnings' with staff members who have simply made a mistake. Often, we can trace the problem back to a corporate policy directive, where staff members are obliged to follow P&C policies, and diverging outside them is simply not acceptable. But it is not simply the fault of the P&C team. Admittedly, they should be at the forefront of developing a healthy culture of coaching and learning within an organisation, and they should be the ones advocating a measured approach to the application of people management. However, let's face it, P&C teams are invariably busy. By the time they are pulled into a performance issue, it is usually late in the day, and they will simply pull out of their bag of policies and procedures something that is going to do the job in a quick and easy way.

Coaching someone once, twice or three times takes time, thought, care and attention. Showing staff members the exit is quicker and easier, but it is not what Jesus would do.

The importance of honest conversations over performance

There is a story about a CEO, named Eddie, who met with a work colleague, Charles, over an early morning coffee. At the end of their meeting Charles announced, 'I have to go and have a "first and final" meeting with Fred, one of my team.'[1]

'Oh,' Eddie replied, 'what's the issue?', thinking that the matter must be very grave.

'Well, he sent off a formal document to the regulator without getting it signed by the proper authorised person.'

'Did he do that deliberately? Did he mean to do it?' Eddie asked.

'No,' said Charles, beginning to feel uneasy. 'But this is the course of action that HR advised.'

'Well,' replied Eddie, 'wouldn't it be better to sit down and have a chat, and coach Fred on this?'

And that is what happened on this occasion.

---

[1] A performance meeting where a staff member is served with a formal warning letter confirming what occurred was unacceptable and the outcome is a final warning. Further infringements could lead to termination.

We have noticed that poor performance-management policies are often linked to a disturbing tendency within many Christian organisations to not tell the truth. As one experienced executive commented to us about two Christians organisations she had worked in:

> One of the most significant and systemic patterns I saw in both of these organisations was a lack of transparency and preparedness for truth-telling in performance management. Culturally it felt like no-one wanted to have the hard conversation around lack of performance, and as a consequence there was behind-the-back criticism and dishonouring of people. How organisationally were we caring for these people, loving them, if we weren't able to have an honest conversation with them, provide them with support, help for them to develop, grow or move to a new role or potentially exit? It created a very unhealthy culture. The whole Christian 'being nice' actually wasn't very Christ-like at all.[2]

Being nice, that is, until the staff member is fired!

This is, of course, a pattern not reserved for Christian organisations; it is a time-honoured cultural flaw in churches and congregations the world over. Yet telling the truth should be a mark of any organisation to whom the name of Christ is attached. In the words of Ephesians 4:15: 'Instead, *speaking* the *truth* in love, we will grow to become in every respect the mature body of him who is the head, that is, Christ.'[3]

The vital role of confession

We have been talking about the importance of forgiveness and honest conversations, but often confession comes before forgiveness. 'If we confess our sins, he is faithful and just and will forgive us our sins ...' (1 John 1:9).

---

2 Email to Stephen Judd (name withheld), 13 December 2020.
3 Italics added.

These words should ring in the ears of the board members and executives of Christian organisations. Organisations, Christian or not, should encourage staff members to own up to mistakes and failures without fear of punishment, and that's because – apart from being biblical – it is the smart operational thing to do. All of us learn more from our mistakes and failures than our successes. Or at least we should. And there is another reason why it is smart to encourage staff to be forthcoming about mistakes and failures: it reduces the risk of nasty surprises.

We know of a large multinational health organisation with annual revenues in excess of $US10 billion that terminated local managers if their service failed an external compliance review by the regulator. At least that is how it appeared to middle management. There might not have been an explicit policy to that effect, but it certainly seemed to the middle managers that being sacked was the price they would pay for failure.

How is that approach supposed to build a quality system, or discourage cover-ups at the local level, or encourage transparency? It does not. All that occurs with such a nonsensical approach is that the senior management and board receive nasty surprises, hearing too late from the media or the external regulator of significant problems that the local manager had probably been furiously and unsuccessfully trying to fix or bury.

Other organisations might not be so punitive, but too often they might make confessions difficult. With them, mistakes and failures are met with excoriation, humiliation, embarrassment or exclusion.

A radical alternative perspective is to develop an organisational culture that not only encourages owning up to mistakes and failures among its staff but even celebrates them. We do not mean a celebration that in some way encourages repeat offending; nor do we mean a celebration that shrugs off the consequences of failing both for the person and the organisation. Rather, think of it is an opportunity to review what has happened, learn from it and improve.

Sports teams understand this approach. Have you noticed that when a player makes a mistake – for example, a dropped ball, a missed tackle – their teammates don't shun them. Rather, they rush in and encourage the player. They are not doing this because they are happy that the mistake has been made, but they know that the best way to lift the team's performance is by acknowledging the error and encouraging the player, rather than punitive action.

Such an approach is anathema to much of our modern work culture, which frequently shows people the door for the first offence. This is such a contrast to the way God deals with us, as the verse from 1 John 1:9 quoted earlier demonstrates. Christian organisations need to be countercultural and distinctive in the ways they manage the mistakes and failings of their staff and teams.

The right seat on the bus

Sometimes forgiveness is expressed in finding 'the right seat on the bus' for staff members. An example is John Nadjarian, a nurse with more than 40 years' experience, particularly when it came to working with older people exhibiting the behavioural and psychological symptoms of dementia.

For 15 years he was the Special Care Program Manager at a nursing home that supported those who were most affected by dementia. His blokey exterior belied his deep concern for the elders in his care: he would make sure that the women had clothes and hairdos that make them feel good about themselves; he would make sure the physically aggressive Alfredo who had worked all his life in a market garden was given tools to work with the maintenance men in the garden. When things went wrong, there was no-one better to be at the frontline. John led by example, modelling to the direct care staff how they were serving people to whom they should relate as people, not a patient with a disease. 'We are people caring for people,' he used to say.

However, John had not always succeeded. Twenty-five years earlier, he was the manager of another nursing home institution, serving some of the most challenging of residents with dementia. The role of a manager of a nursing home is complex and multitasked: appropriate resident admission, staff recruitment and management, relative liaison, managing rosters and finances, and so on. As a hands-on 'do-er', John was failing in this administrative role, and it was showing in outcomes: relatives were unhappy, resident incidents were increasing, there were staff issues and a poor financial performance.

John's boss at that time was an experienced clinician. She could have let him go … but she didn't. She didn't give up on him, nor did she ignore the failings. Rather, she spoke frankly to him about the need for change.

Thinking imaginatively, she offered John a new role that met the emerging needs of the organisation. For the next 10 years, John was in charge of night-time care, a hands-on role that played to John's strengths. His appointment and service resolved many of the concerns about how to improve the quality of care for 300 residents at nights.

It was an inspired change that found the right seat on the bus for John, while also helping the organisation improve its performance. It was also the bridging position to John's next role as one of Australia's finest managers of people with significant behavioural and psychological symptoms of dementia.

Forgiveness is at its finest when it is a 'win-win'.

Review questions

1. What stops us from having honest conversations about performance?
2. How do we balance judgement, mercy and forgiveness?
3. What benefit is there to an organisation that encourages its team members to confess to mistakes and errors?

9. What does redemption look like in organisations?

The Bible, far from being a chronicle of the exploits of successful all-conquering people, is more about stories about how frail and broken people are, how people stuff up, particularly in their relationships with each other. Most outstanding men and women in the Bible seem to have had some sort of experience with brokenness. It almost seems to be the prerequisite for God to work with any of them.

Consider the apostle Peter, a loyal and enthusiastic follower of Jesus. When the soldiers came to arrest Jesus in the Garden of Gethsemane, Peter did not hesitate to whip out a sword and cut off the ear of one of the arresting party. Earlier, he had proudly claimed that he would never disown Jesus (Matt 26:34–35). However, within 24 hours, under pressure, he cracked and denied Jesus – not just once but three times.

Sometime later, after Jesus' death and resurrection, Jesus met the disciples at the Sea of Galilee. Jesus took the issue of Peter's denials head on, then reinstated him. Countering Peter's three denials, Jesus deliberately asked him three times to affirm his love and loyalty to Jesus.

We love this story of Peter. It is a great comfort. It shows how there is a way back to relationship with God even when we stuff up big time. It is an illustration of how redemption is possible. God is the God of not only a second chance but *yet another* chance, as the Old Testament characters King David and Jonah would affirm. As the prophet Micah says, 'Who is a God like you, who pardons sin and forgives the transgression of the remnant of his inheritance?' (Mic 7:18).

Unfortunately, this pattern of redemption is not always found in Christian organisations. This is highlighted especially in recruitment. It seems to us that most Christian organisations would, in today's world, disqualify from employment Old Testament patriarchs like Abraham who pimped and trafficked his wife Sarah – twice! (Gen 12 and 20). Nor would they consider Abraham's grandson, Jacob, a habitual liar and fraud (Gen 27). Indeed, the personnel records would probably say 'do not under any circumstances employ this family!' Why? The reason is simple: those doing the recruiting simply don't want to take the risk. Even though God takes risks with us.

People with baggage

'I have a friend who is just out of prison who needs a job.' With these words the manager got the CEO's attention. The manager went on to explain that his friend James had been in prison for two years and now needed a job.

James had been the finance director of a company that went broke. He had been subsequently convicted of offences related to him issuing documents in which there were material omissions, which had put a rosier gloss on the financial performance of the company.

The CEO read the transcripts of the legal proceedings and interviewed James. After consideration, he authorised James' appointment to a junior role in the organisation's accounting team.

Later, as James' contribution to the organisation became more and more valued, the CEO was asked to authorise James' promotion to a position which would interact with the board. After further consideration he approved the new appointment.

At the next board meeting, the CEO advised directors of James' appointment. Not all board members were happy: concerns about possible reputational damage were voiced. Another made the comment that 'past behaviour is the only indicator of future behaviour.' The CEO's pause button was not on, and he replied, 'In which case we are all condemned!'

And there's the rub. Christians readily acknowledge the words of Paul that 'all have sinned and fall short of the glory of God' (Rom 3:23), but too they often confine the implications of that statement to an individual's personal relationship with God. In fact, Paul's words have more profound implications for how Christian organisations should operate.

Would you hire him?

In 2017 the government of the Australian state of New South Wales launched a public enquiry into the state branch of the Returned and Services League (RSL) as well as RSL LifeCare, its retirement village and aged-care organisation. The enquiry was sparked by allegations in the media of misuse of credit cards and other anomalies at the state branch level and that the directors of RSL Lifecare had paid themselves consultancy fees in contravention of the charitable fundraising regulations. Justice P.A. Bergin SC was appointed to head the enquiry.

By the time Justice Bergin handed down her report in February 2018, a new broom had been put through the council of the state RSL and a new chair appointed. The same thing happened at the RSL's aged care organisation, LifeCare. Justice Bergin found no evidence that the RSL LifeCare directors conducted themselves dishonestly. Rather, she found they had relied on the 'wrong-headed' advice of their honorary legal adviser and that RSL LifeCare's auditors were in part responsible for non-compliance with the Act. However, she determined that the RSL LifeCare board had been 'riddled with conflicts' as they approved their own contracts and consulting fees. As for the CEO of RSL LifeCare, someone who had turned around its financial fortunes, improved its clinical quality and regulatory compliance record, and grown the organisation significantly, Bergin found his conduct was honest and he 'did as much as he could for the best interest of RSL LifeCare.' She said:

> It is very unsatisfactory that a CEO of an organisation should have been placed in the position to which (he) was placed.

> He was the only person to identify the conflict of interest. He took legal advice ... He then took further legal advice in respect of the steps that he took in going about determining the fees. He made an attempt to put some maths around the retainers ... That conduct was honest and was an attempt to bring some rigour to the process.[1]

Bergin's conclusion was small comfort for the CEO: by the time Bergin's report was released, he had parted ways with RSL LifeCare.

So, the question is: with that history, would you hire him?

It might take more courage to trust or offer forgiveness or redemption, but we believe that it is more honest to address the issue of an under-performing manager rather than simply firing them. We argue that while it takes more time and effort, it is much better to have people confess to shortcomings. It also instils confidence at all levels that better performance is being achieved by empowerment rather than concealment for fear of retribution. It produces a more enabling and open culture and thereby a more efficient operational environment. Christian or not, we cannot adopt an approach that skilled personnel are disposable. There is simply not an endless supply of them.

---

1 Department of Finance, Services and Innovation, 'Report of the Inquiry under the Charitable Fundraising Act 1991 into The Returned and Services League of Australia (NSW Division) ... RSL LifeCare Limited', Parliament of New South Wales, January 2018, pp. 441–442, online at https://www.parliament.nsw.gov.au

There may be perceived risk in the application of redemption in hiring people who have 'baggage', particularly if that history is publicly known. However, the benefits far outweigh any actual risk. You are hiring someone who will invariably prove to be a loyal worker and contributor, whose skillset and experience far exceeds the cost.

Forgiveness and redemption are not simply core biblical principles that should be integral to a Christian organisation's theology. They also make good business sense: you grow a loyal workforce, and you develop a workforce that is encouraged to be courageous, that is innovative and tries things that may or may not succeed, knowing that failure is not met with a punitive response.

Review questions

1. Is it true that ideas like forgiveness and redemption are not found in many human resource policies. Why do you think that is true?

2. Do you think that forgiveness and redemption have a place in Christian organisations? Why or why not?

3. What benefit is there to an organisation that encourages its team members to confess to mistakes and errors?

4. In this chapter we asked the question whether you would hire the person with 'history' or 'baggage'. Would you? Why or why not?

SECTION 3

Theological Foundations for Practice

In section 1 we established that Christian organisations, and Christians influencing organisations, are tested by their faithfulness to God's mission. Measures of faithfulness include ethos, identity and the impact of the organisation.

We also talked about the need for organisations to develop an organisational theological statement that governs behaviour.

Section 2 included some foundational ideas concerning sin, judgement, grace, faith, hope, trust, forgiveness and redemption. These are all familiar theological terms for Christians.

In section 3 we introduce some less familiar theological concepts: risk, stewardship and radical hospitality.

10. Being Christian can be risky

Elements such as grace, forgiveness, redemption and judgement are characteristics whose presence in an organisational theological framework should not surprise readers. There are others that just might surprise some, but they shouldn't. Take, for example, an organisation's approach to risk.

A theology of risk

From early in the Bible, it is clear that being in relationship with God invites risk into your life! Take, for example, the story of Abraham.

Abraham's father, Terah, had travelled with his family from Ur in southern Mesopotamia to Harran, where they settled in what is now modern Turkey. After Terah died, God spoke to Abraham: 'Go from your country, your people and your father's household to the land I will show you' (Gen 12:1). Abraham's family is comfortable and established in Harran, but he's told to leave it behind and go into the unknown, to a distant place called Canaan. So, at the ripe old age of 75, Abraham left 'as the LORD had told him' (Gen 12:4). 'By faith Abraham, when called to go to a place he would later receive as his inheritance, obeyed and went, even though he did not know where he was going' (Heb 11:8). If that is not risky, we do not know what is!

In Matthew's Gospel, we are told the story of the disciples being on a boat on Lake Galilee when Jesus walks across the water towards them (Matt 14:27–31):

> But Jesus immediately said to them: 'Take courage! It is I. Don't be afraid.'
> 'Lord, if it's you,' Peter replied, 'tell me to come to you on the water.'
> 'Come,' he said.

> Then Peter got down out of the boat, walked on the water and came towards Jesus. But when he saw the wind, he was afraid and, beginning to sink, cried out, 'Lord, save me!'
>
> Immediately Jesus reached out his hand and caught him. 'You of little faith,' he said, 'why did you doubt?'

The Bible is full of stories of individuals taking risks, in faith. Indeed, they only encounter strife when fear replaces faithfulness.

How does this apply to Christian organisations? We would argue that how an organisation approaches risk is an indicator of its faithfulness.

Risky faithfulness

A more recent example of risky faithfulness is the story of Robert Hammond. For much of the first half of the 20th century, Robert Hammond was the Anglican minister at St Barnabas Broadway in inner-city Sydney. From that parish church, through the Great Depression of the late 1920s, Hammond ran the largest social-service relief organisation in Sydney. However, it was at the age of 61, in 1932, that Hammond embarked on his greatest adventure and took an even greater risk. Cashing in his own life assurance policy (the equivalent today of our superannuation or pension plan), he bought land on the outskirts of Sydney to begin a settlement scheme for destitute families who had been evicted, or were threatened with eviction, from their rented homes.

It was a risky venture. The land he had bought was miles from the nearest town. There were no utilities, no roads, no services. He had no financial backing at the time to complete the task, instead relying on volunteer labour from unemployed men to build the 'pioneer homes'. He met with opposition from the local shire council and rural landowners, who (quite understandably) suspected that this settlement of inner-city unemployed families would be a breeding ground for communist sentiment during the Depression years. However, Robert Hammond dared to fail ... and succeeded. The suburb Hammondville – and the charity HammondCare – was born, and

Hammondville proved to be one of the few successful land settlement schemes in Australia's history.[1]

What is it about the sheer gutsiness of old guys like Abraham and Bob Hammond?

Risk aversion

Christian organisations struggle with the issue of risk. On the one hand, risks were taken to start most of them in the first place. And they were probably established to do things that businesses and governments did not do or would not do: hospices for the dying, caring for the poor and needy, ministering to the physical and spiritual needs of First Nations and immigrant peoples. When you come to think of it, most of them were established to *take on* risk!

But as these organisations grow and their financial and human resource issues become more complex, the founding faithful Christian vision and entrepreneurialism begins to sound a little cavalier for new board members and managers. For many of them, 'risk management' ends up being a euphemism for furious attempts to eliminate all risk.

Too many risk management strategies are in reality 'risk aversion' approaches. They are reinforced by those who invariably become board members of the Christian organisation as it grows: solid, pew-sitting actuaries, accountants, lawyers and the like who have a predisposition to being conservative rather than entrepreneurial.

Moreover, these professionals too often have limited expertise in what the Christian school or welfare organisation actually does. And, what understanding they do have is invariably from the perspective of the commentary box rather than the playing field. Then, because they are not

---

1 Lake, *Faith in Action*; Judd, Robinson & Errington, *Driven by Purpose*, p. 146. Stephen Judd was Chief Executive of HammondCare from 1995 to 2020.

familiar with the environment, such board members become even *more* cautious, conservative and concerned about attendant risks. An inevitable outcome occurs all too often: Board or governance handbooks are developed or updated that are replete with mentions of financial risk, cyber and IT risk, business continuity risk, insurance, and compliance risks. While there might be a mention of Christian motivation and purpose, the discussion of risk management is invariably based on a secular framework and not on a theology of risk.

Rocket Park

An approach to risk within Christian organisations that is devoid of theology reflects the secular culture in which we live; a culture which seeks to minimise or avoid risk. An illustration of this is the proposed intention of a local council in Melbourne, Australia, to remove a rocket from a playground in a park in the suburb of Hawthorn. Yes, a rocket. While the official name of the park is Central Park, all the locals know it as 'Rocket Park'.

As columnist Duncan Fine in *The Age* newspaper explains:

> I'm showing my age but when I was young, every kid wanted to be an astronaut … Stoical, inspirational astronauts were perfectly happy to risk their lives, sitting on top of what was basically a giant firework, blasting off into space and eventually setting foot on the moon.

> In response, down here on earth, local councils all over Australia constructed rocket ships in playgrounds. Like millions of kids, I willingly accepted the challenge of climbing up the series of ladders to the top, admiring the view and then slipping down the slide.

> Now Boroondara Council may remove the iconic rocket in Central Gardens in Hawthorn. Residents are fired up about the plans with one, quite rightly, likening its significance to the neon-lit Skipping Girl sign in Abbotsford.

> We are all sadly used to this now. Officious bureaucrats and lawyers somehow find a way to simultaneously wag their fingers while thumbing their way through voluminous Occupational Health and Safety laws. They then earnestly pronounce that these dangerous structures have no place in a modern playground; preferring instead ones where no child is ever allowed to graze their knee and all fun must be had in a strictly and carefully regulated manner.[2]

At the time of writing, Stephen Judd's four-year-old grandson, Joshua Judd, together with other Hawthorn residents, have been fighting to save their rocket. (Protest and outrage apparently run in the family.)

And it's not just the bureaucracy of local councils. Company directors throughout the world are besieged by endless discussions of risk by their professional bodies. Not a month goes by when they are not encouraged, nay commanded, to attend workshops and courses on IT, HR, financial, cyber, health, safety and myriad other risk issues, else they be found negligent in their duties as directors. Such a fearful consequence strikes fear in the heart of those professional types who have found themselves on the board of a Christian organisation. Being sued or disgraced or worse is not what they counted on when they volunteered to join that board!

Risk management

Some readers might think that we are not taking the issues of risk management seriously. We want to reassure you that we do take risk seriously, and every Christian organisation should. However, what is key is the *management* of risks within the context of the chosen activity of the organisation. True management of risk means that you recognise its enduring presence,

---

2 Duncan Fine, 'Hawthorn, we have a problem', *The Age*, 24 February 2021. The protest was successful, and the local council backed down in June 2021 from its proposal to demolish the rocket.

not engage in a futile 'whack a mole' process to extinguish it. True manage-ment of risk means that the presence of risk is one factor among many in decision-making.

Far from making light of risks, Christian organisations should be exemplars of taking risk management seriously. To that extent, Christian organisations should be highly professional in their incident and risk management systems, and in their determination to proactively identify, measure and engage in risk, in order to meet the needs and preferences of the people that they serve. They should have a deep appreciation that they are seeking to manage risk in an intelligent and measured way, not simply trying to eliminate risks in a futile way. A couple of examples follow.

Interserve

Interserve describes itself as an 'international community of disciples of Jesus Christ.' Its 800 'partners' are doctors, teachers, carpenters, agricultural scientists, community development workers, and many more, who 'share the calling to join God's redeeming and reconciling work in all of creation.' The partners pursue their calling among the peoples of Asia and the Arab world 'by growing as and nurturing disciples, seeking lives and communities transformed through encounter with Jesus Christ.'[3] It is gutsy work and certainly not for the faint-hearted or those prone to chronic homesickness.

Interserve knows about risk and takes it very seriously. It has thought about it deeply, and it is one of the few organisations that has articulated a Theology of Risk applicable to the ministry and mission. Its Theology of Risk statement stands as a challenge to all Christian organisations:

We accept that our calling brings with it certain risks such as

---

3 'About Interserve', n.d., https://interserve.org.au/learn/about/

increased exposure to sickness in countries with less medical facilities than most of our home countries, instability in our living conditions, loneliness and potential trauma for our families and children. While as a responsible organisation we will consider these risks in the decision making of the placement, care and support of our Partners, *they will not solely determine either our placement or our ministries*. We recognise that in many of our countries, the name of Christ is not honoured and any association with it carries the risk of specific targeting for ridicule, suffering and even death. When this happens we will embrace it (following the way of our Saviour).[4]

And there's the rub: risk management must only be one consideration among many. If it becomes the sole or primary determinator within a Christian organisation, it will gradually and inevitably strangle or stifle the organisation's distinctive ministry and purpose.

The Church Missionary Society of Australia

The Church Missionary Society of Australia (CMS-A) is another organisation that has a well-articulated theology of risk. It begins with the statement: 'Our understanding and management of risk is based on a theology of the sovereign God deploying his witnesses in a risky world, until Jesus returns.' It also has a well-analysed risk register that it actively reviews. This register identifies not simply 'secular' risk issues such as loss of key personnel, but theological risks and risks associated with loss of vision, thoughtfully identifying actions to mitigate the identified risks.

Its risk management policy is based on a deeply theological foundation and acknowledges the following:

---

4 Interserve, 'Theology of Risk and Suffering', unpublished document. Emailed to Stephen Judd in September 2020. Italics added.

- God is sovereign and faithful
- CMS members and missionaries entrust themselves to him
- Jesus' great commission to make disciples is a call to 'costly and sacrificial witness'
- God's children are not immune from the risk of living in a broken world
- there is a spiritual war going on, and 'spiritual attacks and oppression' should be expected.[5]

There is no pulling punches here. A clear theological framework for risk, like this one, provides the context and groundwork for the development of a risk register that covers anticipated risks and outlines strategies for managing those risks. It works for the following reasons:

- it recognises upfront that *God* is sovereign, not the CEO or the board of directors
- disciples of Jesus should expect things to go wrong and shape their risk register accordingly
- it acknowledges that there is a spiritual war going on, which means that the best endeavours that are humanly possible will be confounded.

And, in that respect, it matters not what happens, but how Christians – and the organisation within which they serve – respond to what they are confronted with.

The right theology of risk for the organisation

An organisation's theology of risk cannot and should not be simply picked up and applied to all other Christian organisations. For example, Interserve's Theology of Risk statement covers not only risk but an acknowledgement that its partners may indeed suffer in the countries in which they are placed.

[5] Church Missionary Society of Australia, 'Risk Management Policy', unpublished document, Sydney, August 2019.

Quoting Dietrich Bonhoeffer, Interserve's statement says:

> Discipleship means allegiance to a suffering Christ, and it is therefore
> not at all surprising that Christians should be called on to suffer.[6]

The full statement is called a Theology of Risk and Suffering, which would, in our view, be inappropriate to apply to a Christian school, for example!

In the contemporary world, Christian organisations must develop their own Theology of Risk statement. That of the Christian pension fund will look different to the overseas aid agency, which in turn will have a different perspective to a missionary organisation. Similarly, the part that the risk statement plays in the organisational theology of the Christian retirement village operator will be very different to that of the Christian hospital or homeless service. We suspect that Christian entrepreneurs will have a better understanding of risk, but they will need to consider how a theology of risk applies to their organisation once it becomes more established.

What should be common to all Theology of Risk statements is that they are all rooted in the mind of Christ, not the prevailing perspectives of the culture or the business world in which they inhabit. They must all be resolutely countercultural. If an organisation is to bear the name of Christ, they must reflect the same approach to risk as Christ:

> Who, being in very nature God,
>   did not consider equality with God something to be used to his
>   own advantage;
> rather, he made himself nothing
>   by taking the very nature of a servant,
>   being made in human likeness.
> And being found in appearance as a man,
>   he humbled himself
>   by becoming obedient to death –
>   even death on a cross! (Phil 2:6–8).

6 Interserve, 'Theology of Risk and Suffering'.

Review questions

1. Why do you think Christian organisations struggle with risk?

2. Do you agree that this struggle is rooted in our secular culture?

3. What are your thoughts on the theology of risk from CMA-A's Risk Management Policy?

4. What might a theology of risk look like in your organisation?

5. Why should Christian organisations be exemplars of risk management?

11. Stewardship: acknowledging God in all things

'The LORD God took the man and put him into the garden of Eden to work it and take care of it' (Gen 2:15).

From the very beginning of the Bible, we are instructed to be good 'stewards' of God's creation. This stewardship is very much about acknowledging that it is God's creation, not our plaything to do with as we please. As managers of God's creation, we are not to abuse that position for our own advantage but rather remember that it is God who makes everything possible. It is God who creates wealth and gives us whatever material possessions we might have (Deut 8:17–18).

This is not an excuse to be idle, however. The Bible criticises those who are lazy (Prov 10:5; 12:11) and praises those who are honest and act faithfully with others (2 Kgs 12:15). In the book of Leviticus, for example, the people of Israel are instructed by God to be trustworthy in their dealings with others: 'Do not use dishonest standards when measuring length, weight or quantity … I am the LORD your God, who brought you out from the land of Egypt' (Lev 19:35–36). Just as our God is a God of relationships, we are to reflect his character in being trustworthy and honest in our relationships with others.

In the New Testament, the concept of stewardship broadens to include our diligence in using the abilities that God has given us: 'From everyone who has been given much, much will be demanded; and from the one who has been entrusted with much, much more will be asked' (Luke 12:48).

But it broadens even further to encompass the faithful proclamation of the good news of Jesus. Paul writes, 'This, then, is how you ought to regard us: as servants of Christ and as those entrusted with the mysteries God has revealed.

Now it is required that those who have been given a trust must prove faithful', adding that the Lord 'will expose the motives of the heart. At that time each will receive their praise from God' (1 Cor 4:1–2, 5). Paul is making the point that we need to be working for God and not for our own prestige or advantage.

And, again, in Paul's second letter to Timothy: 'Guard the good deposit that was entrusted to you – guard it with the help of the Holy Spirit who lives in us' (2 Tim 1:14).

From all of this we can conclude that stewardship for the Christian is about:

- actively honouring the trust that God has given us to look after his creation
- acting honestly and fairly in our dealings with others
- being forthright and faithful in proclaiming the hope that is in us, namely the good news of Jesus.

Stewarding proactively versus reactively

What is so extraordinary is that this conclusion is so very different to how the idea of stewardship is typically used in Christian organisations. In our experience in Christian organisations, the focus of stewardship almost entirely revolves around financial resources and their allocation. Too often you hear – or hear about – Christian board members saying about a proposal that involves money: 'Oh, we can't do that ... we have to be good stewards of our resources.' We know of one well-resourced Christian organisation that declined to invest its own resources in a project for the poor and homeless on the basis of that very explanation.

However, there is very little biblical support for the idea that the Christian organisation should be conservative and risk averse in their use of material resources, including money. Jesus was not exactly proposing a conservative approach to money when he told the rich young ruler: 'Go, sell your possessions and give to the poor, and you will have treasure in heaven. Then come, follow me' (Matt 19:21). This radical approach is reinforced in the story Jesus tells of the fearful servant who, rather than risk losing the money that had been entrusted to him, goes and buries it: 'So I was afraid and went out and hid your gold in the ground. See, here is what belongs to you' (Matt 25:25).

This is very challenging for us, not simply as individuals, but also as organisations. How often do those of us within Christian organisations appear to be more afraid of losing money or failing financially than doing something that so obviously advances God's kingdom? How often do we decline or defer to express God's love to his creation because we are afraid and, instead, 'bury the gold'? 'Gold' that is not ours but given to us? Does this betray that we are making our decisions not faithfully, based on the mind of Christ, but unfaithfully, based on the world's advice?

The parable of the rich fool in Luke 12 is a warning to us all. A man had a bumper crop and decided to build bigger barns to store the grain. He imagined that he would then be able to sit back and relax:

> But God said to him, 'You fool! This very night your life will be demanded from you. Then who will get what you have prepared for yourself?'
> This is how it will be with whoever stores up things for themselves but is not rich towards God (Luke 12:20–21).

It would be much wiser for Christian organisation to use their funds faithfully to advance the kingdom rather than build bigger barns. They should be more afraid of failing God than failing financially. In that respect, it is heartening to hear words such as those of the treasurer of CMS-A: 'In our finance discussions money does not come first ... everything we do is in the context of our theology.'[1]

---

1 Geoff Girvan, interview with Stephen Judd, 5 March 2021.

Theology first is not conservative

We can be encouraged that God rewards such faithfulness. We know of one Christian health organisation that lost government funding for a palliative care service. Rather than winding down the service that the community depended on, the organisation continued the service at a significant loss. Within a short space of time an unexpected bequest filled the financial gap, and within two years, the government subsidy was restored. Another organisation caring for the homeless made a decision to provide a service that, by any secular financial measure, did not meet investment hurdles. Their faithfulness was met with an abundance of philanthropic support that met their capital needs. In the mid-1990s, when Rosemary Bond was the Director of Care at HammondCare, they built The Meadows, their first purpose-built residential home for people with dementia with three small cottages for 40 residents. In the planning there was lots of thought about what was best for residents with dementia but not much consideration of financial metrics like the project's Internal Rate of Return (IRR) – there is doubt the IRR was even calculated. Twenty-five years later, the IRR over that period was the highest of all the projects that HammondCare had ever undertaken.

A theology-first approach towards stewardship – such as that described at CMS-A – will be reflected differently in each organisation according to its own particular context. A pension fund will apply the concept of stewardship differently to, say, a camping organisation: the former will focus on preserving and growing the retirement nest eggs of its members, but hopefully act with generosity and compassion to the individual circumstances of members; the Christian camp group will focus on caring for the campers and sharing the good news of Jesus with them. Both expressions of stewardship are faithful and bold.

Stewarding creation well

Stewarding God's creation clearly implies caring for the planet as well as people, although Christians in the past may have emphasised 'ruling' and 'subduing' rather than 'caring' and 'protecting'. Paul's inclusion of creation as subject to sin and needing redemption certainly widens the arena of Jesus' activity, and that of his followers:

> For the creation waits in eager expectation for the children of God to be revealed. For the creation was subjected to frustration, not by its own choice, but by the will of the one who subjected it, in hope that the creation itself will be liberated from its bondage to decay and brought into the freedom and glory of the children of God.

> We know that the whole creation has been groaning as in the pains of childbirth right up to the present time. Not only so, but we ourselves, who have the firstfruits of the Spirit, groan inwardly as we wait eagerly for our adoption to sonship, the redemption of our bodies (Rom 8:19–23).

Biblical stewardship also infers that Christian organisations should be leading the way in establishing environmental sustainability policies. Today, in the days of reporting on ESG – Environmental, Social and Governance – it is perhaps not just easier but culturally desirable to report on how an organisation has a lower carbon footprint, greener workspaces, improved waste management and recycling, and so on. This is a welcome development.

One of us (Stephen) shamefully admits that in his 25 years as a CEO there were occasions when he deferred capital expenditure that would have improved the organisation's environmental impact because it was a poor or marginal business case financially.

By now we are sure that some readers, perhaps particularly the treasurers, accountants and actuaries, are 'having kittens'! 'We have to act responsibly,' one will say; 'we must act with prudence,' another will proclaim, and so on.

We remind those readers of Vanhoozer's observation that we must apply the 'mind of Christ'[2] to all our decisions, whatever the context. We must put our trust in God prayerfully and faithfully, as well as wisely. We must rely on God and not our barns of grain.

Review questions

1. Stewardship is often referred to as 'prudent and careful use of resources'. Yet the Bible says stewardship is actively honouring the trust God has given us to look after his creation, act honestly and fairly with others, and be forthright in proclaiming the good news of Jesus. In what ways is this a new idea for you?

2. How would the biblical view of stewardship have an impact on how your organisation operates?

3. Do you think that some organisations are more afraid of financial loss or failure than doing something that so obviously advances God's kingdom? What can be done about this?

---

2 Vanhoozer, *The Drama of Doctrine*, p. 2.

12. Practising radical hospitality

It is not overstating it to say that hospitality is a sacred duty for every Christian. Paul simply told Christians to 'practice hospitality' (Romans 12:13). Being hospitable and caring is a characteristic of God, who is a God of relationships. It is an important theme in the Bible, and understandably so because it is about love in action. Our faith is not just 'belief'. It is lived out, and it is expressed in how we treat not only our friends and family, but also complete strangers – including foreigners:

> When a foreigner resides among you in your land, do not ill-treat them. The foreigner residing among you must be treated as your native-born. Love them as yourself, for you were foreigners in Egypt. I am the LORD your God (Lev 19:33–34).

The Psalmist tells us that 'The LORD watches over the foreigner' (Ps 146:9), and as God's people, we are to do the same.

The least of these

Jesus had plenty to say on the subject of hospitality, including his sobering parable of the sheep and the goats that urges his followers to take action to help those in need:

> Then the King will say to those on his right, 'Come, you who are blessed by my Father; take your inheritance, the kingdom prepared for you since the creation of the world. For I was hungry and you gave me something to eat, I was thirsty and you gave me something to drink, I was a stranger and you invited me in, I needed clothes and you clothed me, I was ill and you looked after me, I was in prison and you came to visit me.'

> Then the righteous will answer him, 'Lord, when did we see you hungry and feed you, or thirsty and give you something to drink? When did we see you a stranger and invite you in, or needing clothes and clothe you? When did we see you ill or in prison and go to visit you?'
>
> The King will reply, 'Truly I tell you, whatever you did for one of the least of these brothers and sisters of mine, you did for me' (Matt 25:34–40).

When we show hospitality to the stranger and address the needs of the poor, the hungry and the ill, it is as if we are ministering directly to Jesus.

The importance of hospitality is also a critical takeaway in Jesus' parable of the good Samaritan. To be a neighbour is to show care for those in need, even if they are complete strangers – or even your enemy! (Luke 10:25–37).

The writer of the letter to the Hebrews adds a refrain: 'Do not forget to show hospitality to strangers, for by doing so some people have shown hospitality to angels without knowing it' (Heb 13:2).

Practising radical hospitality in organisations

What does the biblical command to be hospitable mean for Christian organisations? Clearly, it is not simply about being nice!

We are sure that you can think of examples where organisations could be challenged by the command to radical hospitality: the Christian schools charging hefty tuition fees; the hospital organisations whose revenue is dependent on patients who are members of health funds; the Christian retirement village operators who 'sell' a unit for a considerable entry fee.

Whatever their field of endeavour, every Christian organisation should be able to describe how the biblical injunction to be hospitable applies to them. For a fee-paying school, it might be through the intentional development of a bursary fund to benefit students who could not otherwise attend. The principal of one school told us how the mother of a young Aboriginal man, Jim*, made an appointment to see him. She travelled from the country to the city and told of her concern for her boy and asked that he get the opportunity to attend the school. 'It was,' he said, 'a true case of the importunate widow. There was no real choice to make.'[1]

But, the principal observed, the benefits were two-way:

> (Jim) was a powerful Christian witness, saved his holiday job money to assist children in India and visited them, organised his elders to make a gift of aboriginal tools and weapons to give to the school and was an outstanding sportsman. Other boys regarded him highly, and the community of the school was the beneficiary of a wonderful five years.

Another example might be retirement housing. Many retirement villages in Australia operate on a 'loan-licence' arrangement: the incoming resident pays a lump sum as a 'loan' or entry contribution, and in return, the village operator gives the resident a 'licence' to occupy their unit for life. The most profitable approach to occupancy is to insist that all residents pay this upfront lump sum. Some (but not all!) Christian retirement village operators intentionally practise the approach of renting out some units at a modest weekly rate to incoming residents who could not afford lump-sum entry contributions.

One illustration of this is Grace, who had been a long-time missionary in Pakistan before she retired. She finally returned to Australia as poor as the proverbial church mouse. For the next 30 years she paid a small rent for her villa. She was a key member of the retirement village community, blessing others through her hospitality, love and service. Her personal contribution far outweighed any 'entry contribution' that was waived to enable her to join the community.

---

1 Luke 18:1–8. * 'Jim' is a pseudonym.

For many Christian social entrepreneurs, hospitality is as significant a biblical imperative as justice in terms of motivating their innovation. For example, Dinner on the Table, which uses the profits of providing home-cooked meals to everyday people, to provide a woman supporting a child with a disability a free meal service.[2] Be Hers founder Melody Towns is passionate about freeing people trapped in human slavery and does this through awareness programs, supporting partners such as International Justice Mission, and by running a sewing centre for refugee women, providing meaningful employment and an opportunity for socialisation and friendship.[3]

In the health sector, Christian organisations run hospital services in many countries. However, many now serve private patients with health insurance rather than public patients without it. This is a far cry from how many of these same Christian hospitals started out: providing medical care for all comers, regardless of financial circumstances. After all, the root of the word 'hospital' is the same as 'hospitality'!

Some Christian hospitals argue their hospitality is expressed in the provision of pastoral care, the excellence of their services or the research that they do. Others offer public hospital services that receive subsidies from the state, while still others might quietly admit poorer patients who have no private health insurance. However, the question remains for all Christian providers of health and hospital services: how are they distinctive? How does the biblical command to exercise hospitality find expression in their activities? Is it even possible to be exclusive in one's provision of services and be true to that biblical directive?

This is a conundrum for all Christian organisations, whatever sector they may be in. The answers are not simple, but that does not mean they can

---

2 For more information, see https://www.dinneronthetable.com.au/pages/our-impact (accessed 29 May 2022).

3 For more information, see https://behers.org.au/our-impact (accessed 29 May 2022).

be ignored because it is too hard or apparently unprofitable. They must be faithfully addressed. While all Christian charities must be businesslike in order to be charitable, they should not fall into the trap of the fearful servant, recounted in Matthew 25:

> Then the man who had received one bag of gold came. 'Master,' he said, 'I knew that you are a hard man, harvesting where you have not sown and gathering where you have not scattered seed. So I was afraid and went out and hid your gold in the ground. See, here is what belongs to you' (Matt 25: 24–25).

Christian organisations must not hide behind the false excuse of 'stewardship' and prioritise money over faithfulness, or safety and security over ministering to Christ through service to the poor and the 'least of these'. Rather, hospitality must be a thoughtfully intentional element in their organisational theology.

Hospitality is a theological practice

The focus on hospitality in this chapter emerges naturally from our previous reflections on forgiveness, redemption, grace, judgement, risk and stewardship. As we take these theological principles seriously, we become people who do not just act hospitably, but *are* hospitable. Hospitality is a theological *practice*.

It is worthwhile thinking for a moment about what we mean by the term 'practice'. At one level, a practice is something we do. For example, we might practise accounting or law. These are a series of tasks that we learn to achieve whatever goals we might have. But there is a deeper and more theological meaning to the term 'practice'. Every action we take includes within it a theory. Actions are not value neutral; they are deeply theory laden.

Take, for example, the practice of Holy Communion or the Lord's Supper. At one level, it is simply a group of human beings sitting around eating bread and drinking wine. However, when you reflect theologically on these physical actions, you find yourself drawn back into the life, death and resurrection of Jesus. What looks like eating and drinking has an underlying theology that makes it something much deeper, much thicker. Participating in the Lord's Supper has meaning, purpose and a history that transform the action.

Likewise, hospitality is a practice that, when reflected on theologically, reveals deep meanings. As we offer hospitality, we fulfil Jesus's command to

- *love one another*: 'My command is this: love each other as I have loved you' (John 15:12)

- *care for the poor, the widowed and the orphan*: 'Religion that God our Father accepts as pure and faultless is this: to look after orphans and widows in their distress and to keep oneself from being polluted by the world' (Jas 1:27)

- *evangelise the world with God's love*: 'I am sending you out like sheep among wolves. Therefore be as shrewd as snakes and as innocent as doves' (Matt 10:16).

In other words, offering hospitality is a mark of discipleship. This is what makes hospitality radical, because discipleship involves us becoming new creations, transformed by grace; the same gracious welcome we received from God is what we offer to others. Reflection on hospitality's inner depths takes us back to the roots of our faith and drives us into the world in more faithful ways.

Such radical hospitality always has a cost, but it can also lead to long-term, flourishing relationships. Take for example, Charles and Alice, who went on a world tour in 1966. In Jerusalem they were met by George, a Palestinian tour guide with whom they built a strong rapport. George and his wife Maria and eight children lived in the Old City in East Jerusalem, and he knew the sacred sites of Jerusalem very well indeed. The Church of the Holy Sepulchre was the local church that the family attended.

In June 1967, the Middle East erupted into what became known as the Six-Day War between Israel and the forces of Egypt, Syria and Jordan. Before the war, Jerusalem had been divided, with West Jerusalem in Israel and East Jerusalem in Jordan. After the war, all of Jerusalem came under Israeli control. For George, the change was devastating. He, like many other Palestinian tour guides, soon lost their jobs and life became very hard.

Back in Australia, Charles and Alice learned of the plight of George and his family. Charles's family business sponsored the Palestinian family of 10 to Australia, where George was given employment as a handyman and the family accommodation in a weatherboard home nearby. The children went to local schools, took up trades, went into business, and worked in nursing, accounting and other professions. Eventually George retired, and the family moved away and built their lives throughout Australia. A small act of radical hospitality made it possible for generations of George and Maria's family to build lives for themselves in a new land.

Review questions

1. Hospitality is a big theme in the Bible, and it is a practical expression of love. What does the biblical command to be hospitable mean for Christian organisations?

2. Can you give examples of how an organisation you are familiar with is radically hospitable?

3. If hospitality is a theological practice, how is it expressed?

SECTION 4

Keeping It Grounded

We have argued that organisations must be faithful in identity, behaviour and impact to truly be described as Christian. To do this, they need to develop a Statement of Organisational Theology that reflects their particular purpose and context.

As we have developed the concept of organisational theology in this book, we have tried to show the ways in which business practices have hidden depths of meaning that need to be reflected upon theologically if we are truly to develop faithful organisations.

Having suggested some concepts or elements that should be included in an articulated organisational theology, in section 4 we move to a discussion about how these theologies might be developed within organisations.

13. Embedding theology in practice

So far, we have discussed how there is not necessarily a correlation or connectedness between what the individual Christian trustee, board member or manager believes and how an organisation behaves. There are all sorts of reasons for this. It might be because they have not really thought about how their faith is applied to the activities of the organisation. They might have simply assumed that because they and their fellow trustees and board members were Christian, the corporate behaviour would naturally, even osmotically, reflect God's mission. Even if that behavioural expectation was vague, sketchy and unexplained.

Almost certainly these individual believers will have different 'theologies' – different knowledges of God – and it is unlikely these differences will have been discussed or explored. More disturbingly, this dissonance between individual faith and corporate behaviour might be because these believers think that they are constrained by processes and procedures which are more secular than Christian. Worse still, these Christians may have unconsciously parked their faith at the door, keeping it separate from the collective decisions, actions and nature of the organisation.

Bridging the chasm

This chasm between individual faith and corporate practice cannot be bridged by a values statement or a signed Statement of Faith. We have observed that such approaches do not resolve the problem. First, values statements have the effect of quickly taking Jesus out of the picture. Jesus is a person, not a system of moral rules and values. While values statements might point to an overall moral approach to which an organisation adheres or aspires, they do not make the organisation Christian.

Second, Statements of Faith might indicate that the individual is a believer but not much else. It's a little like getting a group of people to affirm their love of football without getting any indication of what team they support or how much they know about the game or, indeed, whether they play the game themselves. Statements of Faith cannot by themselves capture a shared understanding which translates individual belief into collective action.

We contend that the way to resolve this issue – the missing link – is an articulated Organisational Theology, which takes the knowledge of God and details how it applies in every activity of an organisation, be it a school, overseas aid agency, pension fund, health service or whatever. Over the past several chapters, we have identified what elements or components could be included in such a document. However, that's only the beginning. In this chapter we will give three examples of the way an organisation's theology can be brought alive and made real by being embedded into every activity and approach of an organisation.

Only then will organisations be able to function faithfully in fulfilling their part in God's mission to reconcile everything on earth and heaven to himself through Jesus (Col 1:15–20)

People management

If our God is one who values people above all of creation, it follows that how people are treated within an organisation matters, whether it be their recruitment, remuneration, coaching, development, encouragement or discipline. Surely this is the area of an organisation where the mind of Christ should be most evident and where those who are *imago dei* – in the image of

God – are not spoken of in the same way as physical and financial assets, but rather in ways that reflect the way God regards and cares for them.

Yet if you were to look at the human resource or P&C policies of a Christian organisation that you are familiar with, would you find these policies starting with avowedly Christian premises and beliefs?

We have looked at the recruitment and staff performance policies of a number of Christian organisations and discovered the following: first, the recruitment policies usually include a discussion on the need to recruit, the various methods of recruitment and how the remuneration and conditions are calculated. They will detail how candidates are selected, interviews conducted, references checked and offers of employment made. They might conclude by describing how induction and administrative tasks are undertaken for and with the new employee.

The only mention of anything to do with Christ and things Christian may be in a sentence or two in the purpose statement at the beginning of the recruitment policy. The purpose statement of one such policy says its purpose is to ensure good practice in the recruitment of employees who are capable of performing their roles as well as ensuring that the organisation recruits people 'who are aligned with its Christian vision and values'.[1] Aside from that clause, the policy is indistinguishable from that of any secular company. While the clause is commendable, one gets the impression that it is not the first thing that comes to mind when recruitment activities are undertaken.

The same applies in staff performance policies that we have seen. Such policies usually describe how managers provide feedback and coach their staff. So far, so good. However, the bulk of these policies focus on issues like performance management, disciplinary proceedings and termination of

---

1 Recruitment policy of an Australian Christian organisation (name withheld).

employment. While there is plenty of discussion of what amounts to judgement (although it is not put in those terms), there is no mention of the importance of forgiveness and repentance, which we discussed in an earlier chapter. As our God is a God of relationships, and forgiveness for 'trespasses' that fracture our relationship with God and with each other is a core tenet of Christianity, this truth should not only be explicitly articulated in the statements that form a Statement of Organisational Theology, but it should then find expression at the core of policies such as recruitment and performance management.

Christian leadership and the grace of God

Earlier we identified that there is no more central concept in Christian theology than grace. But we also identified that while grace is a freely given gift, there are different views of grace: common grace that is God's mercy and kindness to all of his creation; and special grace, expressed through the death of Jesus, an amazing act of love that demands a response from us.

A Christian organisation's theological statement has to be transparent. It needs to articulate how it sees God's grace expressed and what that means for recruitment, particularly the recruitment of its leaders. If its perspective is primarily one that common grace is the way that God's grace is expressed, then clearly the focus of the leadership of its workforce is to 'do good' and it is less concerned with the personal beliefs of the agents doing that good.

If, however, the organisation's theology emphasises God's special grace, then that will shape the kind of leaders it hires. It will look for people who are forthright and winsome disciples of Christ. A personal faith in Jesus and an ability to declare him as Lord will be intrinsic to the way they think about relationships, community and work. It is because of that personal faith, more than any expertise or experience that they might have, that they are motivated to work in a Christian organisation that gives practical expression to God's love for his creation.

Thus, a well-articulated Statement of Organisational Theology will make clear how the organisation understands what the grace of God means, how that influences its leadership, and therefore how it recruits those leaders.

Embedding a theology of risk into a risk management policy

In an earlier chapter, we discussed how CMS-A has embedded its theology of risk into its risk management policy. We have reproduced the first part of this policy in Appendix 1.[2]

The way CMS-A's theology has been embedded into its risk management policy has been well thought through. Before they dive into a risk matrix or a risk register, they describe their theology of risk. Their theology then drives how the matrix and the register are developed and maintained, as well as their overall management of risk.

This full-blown articulation of a theology of risk might well be alien to many risk managers. It might even induce discomfort among some trustees and board directors. However, this theological statement means that risk management for this organisation starts from an agreed theological standpoint. By grounding CMS-A's risk management policy in a theological statement, CMS-A does more than inform its risk matrix, it profoundly influences its decision-making and its activities.

These three examples – people policies, leadership and risk management – hopefully give an idea of how an organisational theology is not something that gathers dust on a shelf or is buried in the electronic records of the board. Rather, it must find expression in everything that an organisation does. In the next chapter we will look at that process.

---

2 Our thanks to Peter Rodgers, federal secretary, and Geoff Girvan, federal treasurer, of CMS-A for making this excerpt available and for discussing its implementation with us.

Review questions

1. There is no necessary nexus between what an individual Christian believes and how an organisation behaves. What do you think are some of the reasons for this?

2. The authors made the contention that a values statement or a Statement of Faith are poor mechanisms to bridge that gap between individual belief and corporate behaviour. Do you agree? Give reasons for your response.

3. Do the corporate policies of your Christian organisation reflect the mind of Christ? If not, why not?

4. How can an organisational theology be embedded into processes and practices of, say, the people and culture management of an organisation?

5. How can the articulation of an organisational theology inform how and who you appoint as leaders to an organisation?

6. What, if any, policies and procedures of your organisation are based on theological statements? If they aren't, why not?

14. Developing a practical organisational theology

The first thing to say about how one should develop a practical organisational theology is that we don't think you can simply go out and buy one. There should not be 'off-the-shelf' templates. Sure, there will be common elements, and in previous chapters we detailed as many as 12 that could be considered for incorporation. However, these theologies have to be 'owned' by an organisation, and its theological statement must be relevant to its sphere of activity. A school's Statement of Organisational Theology will be different to that of a Christian startup; the private hospital different to that of the homeless service; the pension fund different to that of the welfare organisation, and so on.

Further, the very fact that there are different perspectives, theologies and Christian traditions means that organisational theologies need to be tailored to suit each service. For example, while we admire CMS-A's view of risk as a missionary organisation, a school or a hospital will have a different perspective, even while all are expressing what it looks like to express organisational faithfulness.

So rather than prescribing various templates for your organisational theology, we want to propose three simple steps to follow to develop a statement.

An organisational theology cannot be 'co-designed'

Some organisations might initially be tempted to get a whole range of people into the room to 'workshop' such a statement.

This approach is fraught with danger. As we have discussed before, there might be a wide range of Christian (and perhaps non-Christian) perspectives within such a group. While the apostle Paul has an aspirational hope that, looking forward, we will 'reach unity in the faith' (Eph 4:13), he nevertheless recognises that there are different levels of maturity and knowledge. So, we should not anticipate or expect that 'unity in the faith' will produce agreement. One only needs to look at the interaction of the apostles to see that unity of the faith is not analogous to agreement.[1]

The real danger with the 'co-designed' approach is that in the pursuit of 'consensus', there will be a dilution to the lowest common denominator which will result in statements that are meaningless. James Burtchaell is particularly caustic of his assessment of the end result of such workshops. He concluded that one such document was so impractically vague that it succeeded in 'titrating all previous ... statements into a dilution that contains only trace elements of meaning floating in a sea of solvent.'[2] Ouch!

One of us (Stephen) experienced this peril when he was CEO of HammondCare. In 2004, HammondCare's executive team reviewed its Mission, Motivation, and Mission in Action statements. These three statements each flowed from the other. The Mission statement was a short sentence reflective of the core health and aged care activity of the organisation: 'Our passion is improving quality of life for people in need', a statement that almost all staff could identify with. The Motivation statement proclaimed that the reason for our Mission was

> the Christian principles and values expressed in the words and deeds of Jesus Christ. HammondCare believes in the value of all people as made in the image of God and as loved by God. We are therefore called to show the same love, with compassion and respect, for people in need.

Finally, the Mission in Action statement sought to put these statements into practice, describing what that mission looked like in 15 short sentences about

---

1 Acts 10 and 15; Gal 2:11–14.
2 Burtchaell, *The Dying of the Light*, p. 167.

'how we serve' and 'how we work'. It all fitted on a single page, a single poster and even a wallet-sized fold-out.

In 2004 a group of HammondCare's executives workshopped these three statements. Most of the focus of the workshop was on the Mission in Action part of the document. However, during the workshop's wordsmithing, another executive unobtrusively replaced 'Jesus' with 'God' in the Motivation statement part of the document. The executive's motive was presumably to be 'inclusive' of staff members of other religions as HammondCare had employees of all faiths and none. With all the focus of the workshop on the Mission in Action part of the document, the change was missed. Jesus had dropped out of the picture! It was not until the amended document went to the board for review and approval that a board member noticed and objected to the change and 'Jesus' made it back into the Motivation statement. The organisation owed that board member a debt of gratitude.

Instances such as this one show why the development of an organisational theology statement should be done by *a small group of committed and theologically literate Christians, men and women who have demonstrated the mind of Christ in their decision-making and who clearly seek to mirror and follow Jesus.* Only after that has been done should others within the organisation be engaged and their comments sought on what the smaller group has developed.

Affirming what is – or should be – believed

The task of this small group is to affirm what you believe. Some people might say that affirming what we believe is redundant: 'Cannot we simply agree on the Apostle's Creed and, if necessary, the Nicene Creed? After all, that is what Christians have together affirmed for centuries. Can't we then just get on with our service to our fellow man and woman?'

As we have said earlier, the short answer to this question is 'No'. While that might be true for Christians as individuals, the very fact that there are multiple and diverging denominations implies that there are inescapably different theological positions and perspectives as to how the facts as represented in the Creeds impact on our lives. We ignore those differences at an organisation's peril.

Moreover, from what we have observed, the actual corporate practices within Christian organisations suggest that we are ignoring, setting aside or simply not thinking about the practical application of these beliefs in corporate life. If we are to apply faith into corporate practice, we must write down what we believe. The exercise is in itself valuable and is time well-spent. Perhaps a starting point might be some of the components that we have mentioned earlier in this book – faith and trust, forgiveness and redemption, risk, stewardship, hospitality, and so on. Each organisation might then include aspects that are priorities for them: schools might reflect on their theology of knowledge and learning; an entrepreneurial IT startup might focus on stewardship in how it relates to customers and investors; camping organisations might focus on the beauty of creation and our stewardship of it. The organisational theology of both educational and camping organisations might describe why and how they evangelise. Missionary organisations might spend more time on Christ's Great Commission (Matt 28:18–20) and articulate what it means for them.

Get an experienced professional to assist

When organisations develop internal audit policies, governance manuals, risk registers and the like, they often engage people who are experienced in developing such manuals and policies.

So, it is somewhat confounding to us that when boards or executives come to things like a theological statement or set of statements, the board or chief executive suddenly become DIY – do it yourself. We can make up our own minds whether this is because of ignorance, arrogance or disdain for those who have expertise in this area (such as practical theologians or theologically literate corporate governance types). Or they might be wanting to save a few pennies. But whatever the reason, like so many DIY jobs around the house – at least around our houses – the result is pretty ordinary, or even potentially dangerous!

The exercise of developing an organisational theology goes to the very heart of the organisation's identity and purpose, and it has implications for its future. There is no more important governance task. This is not the time or the place to display arrogance or a false economy, so we strongly recommend getting professional help.

While some elements of the statement might be long, by necessity, mostly you can have a series of short statements. Once these statements are developed – rather than sitting in isolation and neglect on a shelf far removed from the operations – they should be embedded. In this way, they will drive an organisation's policy documents, taking CMS-A's Risk Management Policy as an example.

The development of a Statement of Organisational Theology is a key to attaining and retaining organisational faithfulness, but what about *losing* faithfulness? How does that occur and how can you tell when it is happening? A checklist will follow.

The writer of the letter to the Hebrews challenges us as individual Christians to

> throw off everything that hinders and the sin that so easily entangles. And let us run with perseverance the race marked out for us, fixing our eyes on Jesus, the pioneer and perfecter of faith. For the joy that was set before him he endured the cross, scorning its shame, and sat down at the right hand of the throne of God (Heb 12:1–2).

It is a daunting task to maintain organisational faithfulness. It requires discipline, and a conscious and continuous intentionality. For many, this might seem simply impossible – and perhaps it is – but as Jesus said, 'What is impossible with man is possible with God' (Luke 18:27).

Review questions

1. We recommend three components to the development of an organisational theology:
   - not 'co-designing' the statement
   - affirming what is believed
   - getting an experienced professional to assist.

   How do you respond to each of those ideas? What is missing?

2. What are the dangers of a 'co-designed' statement?

3. In this chapter we contend that a Statement of Faith or an agreement that people attend church is enough to affirm what is believed. Do you agree or disagree?

4. Is it true that there is a gap between individual belief and shared collective behaviour? If so, why do you think that is?

5. Do you agree that bridging that gap is necessary to attain and retain organisational faithfulness?

15. Organisational faithfulness checklist

To this point we have tackled the challenge of Christian organisations remaining faithful to their Christian identity and purpose. We have explored what is too often the yawning gap between what individual Christians believe – be they directors, executives or staff members – and how the organisation itself operates. We have shown how a Statement of Organisational Theology can bridge that gap. We have also described some of the elements that could be included in such a statement that then informs the collective and corporate approaches and actions of the organisation, and is embedded in its practices. We have suggested how such a statement can be developed.

It is by steps such as these that organisational faithfulness can be maintained and flourished.

We now provide the following checklist on how organisations can recognise the warning signs that they are losing their Christian identity and purpose.

The loss of faithfulness

Earlier we quoted Chris Crane of Edify, a global education aid organisation:

> It's the exception that an organisation stays true to its mission. The natural course – the unfortunate natural evolution of many originally Christ-centered missions – is to drift.[1]

This is a gloomy conclusion. How does it happen? How do Christian organisations lose their faithfulness? How can you ensure that your organisation is an exception to Crane's rule? Let us now look at a number of ways an organi-

---

1 Chris Crane, quoted in Greer & Horst, *Mission Drift*, p. 19.

sation loses its faithfulness so that we can be more aware of how to counteract mission drift.

1. A gradual shift

The way an organisation loses its faithfulness is gradual and subtle. In fact, research shows that the shifts and slides – what are, in fact, theological confrontations – are never head on but happen rather subtly, at an angle.[2]

Steps towards faith*less*ness can also happen as much by omission as by commission. We know of one organisation that had a Statement of Faith signed by all of its board trustees, but it was out of sight in the board handbook. When the handbook was revised, the external consultant they engaged consigned the Statement of Faith to an appendix, where it could presumably cause neither offence nor alarm. Nor would it get in the way of the 'professional' approach to governance as prescribed by any secular governance institute.

The lesson is clear: individual and corporate alertness and consciousness are an essential defence against the erosion of organisational faithfulness.

2. Overconfidence

'Pride goes before destruction, a haughty spirit before a fall' (Prov 16:18).

The Bible is full of injunctions about how pride is destructive to relationships and not least our relationship with God. While most of these injunctions are personal, they are also true for organisations. An organisation that proudly thinks it is immune from losing its Christian faithfulness is the one at most risk of doing exactly that. Its pride might not be loud and boastful; it might be simply a quiet, supreme confidence that such a risk is covered and that such a thing will never happen to their organisation, or that the collective attention of the organisation should be on other, more operational matters. If

---

2 Burtchaell, *The Dying of the Light*, p. 169.

that is what people in your organisation believe, the slide has already begun. 'If you believe you are immune, then you are most vulnerable.'[3]

This is even more so when trustees or directors believe that because all the people around the board table are card-carrying Christians, mission drift cannot happen to their cherished organisation. Such confidence is arrogant and not supported by the evidence. The slide to faithlessness doesn't begin and develop pace because of some stealthy infiltration by anti-Christian activists. It begins with Christians around the table and the decisions they make. It gathers pace because of what those Christians pay attention to and what they ignore.[4]

3. The hoax of harmony

In *The Dying of the Light*, James Burtchaell gives examples of how the pursuit of harmony within educational institutions led to a loss of organisational faithfulness. Often it began with a desire not to be 'sectarian'. Burtchaell's research showed that purpose and belief statements that were workshopped over the years showed evidence of a 'repeated inclination to modify, to blur, to compromise … while claiming continuity' and there was increased willingness 'to soften any truth claim if it obstructed any fellowship.' Organisations ended up being 'neither sectarian nor Christian.'[5]

Yet a proper understanding of 'unity in the faith' allows for strong and indeed significant disagreements – even theological ones – among people in relationship with each other through Jesus. In a society that increasingly adopts the paradigm that 'if you disagree with me then you must hate me', this is radically countercultural. However, consider how Jesus operated: he didn't agree with the lifestyle of the woman caught in adultery (John 8:1–11)

---

3 Greer & Horst, *Mission Drift*, p. 90.
4 Burtchaell, *The Dying of the Light*, p. 833.
5 Ibid., pp. 7, 235, 63.

and he didn't agree with Zacchaeus' lifestyle (Luke 19:1–10), but nonetheless he loved them.

The hoax of harmony calls an organisation into disaster. In a desire to secure agreement, we end up with statements that are meaningless gobbledygook. References to 'Jesus' are replaced with references to 'that remarkable if opaque concept "human values" and its equally mysterious affiliate "the Judaeo-Christian heritage."'[6] Eventually any expression of faith must be kept private and most certainly at the periphery of corporate endeavour. By then, the loss of organisational faithfulness is complete.

4. Ignoring the 'Why?'

Every organisation needs to review its operational strategy. The external environment changes, the market and competition change, and the needs of clients and customers also change. However, what is often lost in a strategic review is the 'Why?', the purpose of the organisation. In his 2009 book *Start with Why*, Simon Sinek reflected that while many management consultants and CEOs ask the 'How?' and the 'What?' and only then the 'Why', he reckons the best innovators start with the 'Why?'[7]

Sinek recognised that people join companies because they believe in them. The organisation's identity and purpose, their 'Who?' and their 'Why?', is more fundamental than their 'What?' and 'How?' In fact, employee engagement is derived from the belief that staff members have in a company: 'a strong workplace culture grounded in a rich, engaging sense of purpose is foundational to high-performing organisations.'[8] Research shows for

---

6 Ibid., p. 172.

7 Sinek, *Start with Why*; see also his TED talk 'Start with why – how great leaders inspire action', 29 September 2009, https://www.youtube.com/watch?v=u4ZoJKF_VuA, accessed 12 September 2022.

8 See Louise Parkes' article in *Illuminations*, June 2008, p. 4. *Illuminations* is an e-magazine of the Australian Psychological Society.

example that high-performing charities are those that are driven by purpose, the 'Why?'[9]

Says Peter Greer:

> Knowing who you are is the first line of defence against drift; it allows you to determine if change and adjustments are equipping you to better accomplish your mission or slowly moving you away from your foundation.[10]

Why is there a loss of focus on the 'Why?' One reason is that almost invariably a strategic review is about what financial, physical and human resources are required to achieve growth and improvement. It focuses on the necessary interactions with stakeholders: clients and customers, regulators, funders, investors and supporters, media, government.

When developing any new strategy document, it is therefore helpful to

- check whether a concern for organisational faithfulness is front and centre
- check not only what has been included in the document, but what has been discarded.

Such checks are also useful when there has been a review of other governing documents, particularly Statements of Faith and values statements.

5. The allure of growth

A focus on growth accentuates the tendency to leave the 'Why?' behind. The very success of an original vision results in expansion. The size and reach of the organisation increases, and it becomes more professional, with the skillsets of its workforce developing.

Among the organisation's professionals, there will be practitioners whose allegiance is to their discipline and their careers. They may be the excellent

---

9 Judd, Robinson & Errington, *Driven by Purpose*, especially ch. 5.
10 Greer & Horst, *Mission Drift*, p. 72.

educationalist, the charismatic clinician or the capable development and aid director,[11] but they have no passion for the organisation's purpose. The reason they joined the organisation is that they were attracted to its activities, the 'What?', but they are not aligned with its 'Why?'. The danger is that they will develop into organisational terrorists (see chapter 4) who, seeking to shape the organisation in their own image, will destroy it.

6. Serving two masters

'No one can serve two masters. Either you will hate the one and love the other, or you will be devoted to the one and despise the other. You cannot serve both God and money' (Matt 6:24).

Jesus' teaching here has as much relevance for the Christian organisation as for the individual Christian. A focus on money rather than mission leads a Christian organisation into unfaithfulness.

The heart of a Christian organisation might become apparent if you follow the money. For example, while we believe in the importance of measurements, what are the overriding KPIs for the organisation? Do financial metrics dominate the organisation's thinking, reporting and practice? Christian organisations should be very wary when financial metrics become the determinant of whether missional activity is done – or is not done![12]

One corrective is to measure things that relate more directly to your mission. Are the outcomes of your business practices gauged by faithfulness to the mission of God who gifts, inspires and guides us? Are the business cases over the past year determined primarily by financial metrics or missional imperatives? Is your service to clients shaped by budgets rather than compassion and grace?

The impossibility of serving the two masters can also be experienced when dealing with philanthropic donor and government regulators.

---

11 Examples are given by Burtchaell, *The Dying of the Light*, pp. 147, 178, 224.
12 See an example of this in Judd, Robinson & Errington, pp. 138–139.

7. The seductive donor

Christian organisations often make the mistake of going 'Jesus-lite' in order to meet the needs of a philanthropic supporter.

Peter Greer is the President and CEO of HOPE International, a Christian microenterprise development organisation. Greer tells the story of a meeting he had with a financial supporter in Houston, Texas, who loved what HOPE International was doing. The donor wanted to substantially increase his support, but there was a catch: the donor wanted HOPE to tone down its Christian mission.[13] Greer's experience is not unusual: welfare, overseas aid and health organisations experience this sort of pressure on a regular basis, with philanthropic supporters wanting the good deeds without the Christian motivation. The temptation to acquiesce is enormous. Faced with what Greer terms as the challenge – 'tone down your Christian distinctiveness or forfeit our funding' – Greer graciously declined the donor's support and urges other Christian organisations to do the same.[14]

It is vital that Christian organisations are consistently upfront about their Christian identity and purpose. Actual and prospective supporters can then make an informed decision about whether they will support the organisation's work. Difficulties will almost always occur when supporters are suddenly surprised that the 'do gooders' that they were enthusiastically supporting suddenly – in their eyes – 'come out' as Christians. They feel they have been deceived: this is understandable, and perhaps not always incorrect.

8. Acquiescing to overreach

Another force that can negatively impact upon organisational faithfulness comes from government, either in the form of conditional funding or coercive regulatory requirements.

---

13 Greer & Horst, *Mission Drift*, p. 16.
14 Ibid., p. 18

Starting in the late 1990s, contractual arrangements for government subsidies began including clauses that seek coercively to re-shape the character of a provider organisation. An example are the so-called 'gagging clauses', whereby social services organisations that had been advocates for social improvement and change, and also delivered government-subsidised services, were stifled in their ability to critique government policy by the presence of non-advocacy clauses in their service delivery contracts. Whereas a wealthy philanthropist might want a Christian charity to go 'Jesus-lite', the 'gagging clauses' were designed to stifle criticism of government policy or inaction.[15]

Later, employment regulations and guidelines were proposed that sought to restrict whom Christian organisations could employ, or at least tried to.[16] Then the push was on to direct what procedures Christian hospitals must perform, be they abortion or sterilisation and, more recently, euthanasia.[17]

Similarly, at the very time that there are regulatory standards that *require* provider agencies to support the spiritual needs and not just the physical and emotional needs of the person they seek to care, there is this discordant injunction against 'prosleytising', a corrupted and pejorative term that is seemingly only ever used by those antagonistic to the Christian message.

Assenting to one specific regulatory pressure will not by itself result in a loss of Christian character. However, taken as a whole, meek acquiescence to such pressures will result in the erosion of the Christian character of an

---

15 Joan Staples, 'NGOs out in the cold: Howard Government policy towards NGOs', *UNSW Faculty of Law Research Series*, 2007, Paper 8.

16 Some of these guidelines and regulations are referred to in Patrick Parkinson, 'Christian concerns about an Australian Charter of Rights', *Australian Journal of Human Rights*, vol. 15, no. 2, 2010. See also Australian Human Rights Commission, 'Religious values in employment: Draft Guidelines', 4 August 2000, https://humanrights.gov.au/about/news/media-releases/religious-values-employment-draft-guidelines, accessed 22 July 2022.

17 Judd, Robinson & Errington, *Driven by Purpose*, pp. 9–10; Aleisha Orr, 'Call to dump anti-abortion health provider', *WAtoday*, 16 April 2012, http://www.watoday.com.au/wa-news/call-to-dump-antiabortion-health-provider-20120415-1x18f.html#ixzz22G2hqfYG, accessed 23 July 2012.

organisation. We recommend more robust responses such as deleting the objectionable clauses in contracts and politely but firmly declining demands that the organisation change its spots. The risk is that the organisation will lose a government contract or subsidy, but the alternative is that the organisation loses its integrity.

9. Losing distinctiveness

As much as regulators declare a love for innovation, the reality is that their first love is uniformity. It is so much easier to regulate sectors such as health, aged care, overseas aid and education if all the providers and participants are the same. It makes the task of assessing compliance with standards so much easier.

However, for the Christian organisation, compliance-driven uniformity should be resisted. It undermines any differentiation the organisation might have that is based on its identity and purpose. Its Christian character is lost in an assimilation into the prevailing external culture and it no longer stands out. The very genius of a successful organisational strategy – differentiation – is lost and replaced with a 'same-same' salute to the regulators, who thereby become the new masters of the organisation's destiny. Maintaining and stridently asserting the organisation's Christian identity and purpose is not simply a matter of being organisationally faithful, it is strategically smart.

10. Antipathy towards clergy and theologians

Many Christian organisations were founded by ministers of religion, something that should not surprise us. Rather, we should have an expectation that Christian ministers of religion are in the frontline of participating in God's redemption of the world, and, indeed, the initiative and leadership that these ministers of religion took is often lauded in the histories of these organisations.[18]

---

18 For example, World Vision was established by Robert Pierce, a Baptist minister. Habitat for Humanity was established by Disciples of Christ missionary, Millard Fuller. Many if

However, what is astounding is how, over time, the influence of ministers of religion so sharply diminishes from the ranks of trustees and directors as to become barely consequential. Why is that?

Here are a few suggestions:

- Their knowledge and skills are not deemed to be of primary importance by board chairs or nominations committees.
- Their theological expertise and training are not appreciated.
- There is a fear of church influence.

Whatever the bases for the implicit disdain of clerical candidature for governance of Christian organisations, such bases are flawed for four reasons:

- We are not suggesting that any clergy person is suitable any more than any lawyer or doctor is. That inference is ridiculous. You can have a 'dud' clergy person on the board as much as you have a dud doctor.
- The very fact that so many ministers of religion were the founders of aid agencies, schools, universities and other charities surely says something about the vision and entrepreneurialism of at least those ordained men and women. In fact, they have the very things that we want trustees and directors of Christian organisations to have.
- Clergy have theological qualifications. If an articulation of an organisation's theology is vital to the health and future maintenance

---

not most of the private (non-State) US colleges and universities counted clergy as founding trustees and key influences. The Brotherhood of St Laurence in Melbourne Australia was founded by Father Gerard Tucker, an Anglican priest. Tucker also founded Food for Peace, which became Community Aid Abroad, and now is Oxfam Australia. HammondCare was founded in Sydney Australia by Anglican minister, Rev. RBS Hammond. The various city-based Wesley Missions in Australia were invariably 'superintended' or led by Methodist ministers; and its most famous Australian superintendent, Rev. Sir Alan Walker, established Lifeline in 1963. Similarly, the UK's largest charity care provider, Methodist Homes (now rebranded MHA) was founded by the Methodist minister Rev. Walter Hall. Many of the Catholic health, aged care and welfare organisations were founded by orders of Catholic sisters, such as the Sisters of Mercy and Sisters of Charity.

of a Christian organisation's identity and purpose – and hence its faithfulness – surely it is essential that people with theological qualifications actively contribute at a governance and executive level.

- The published evidence – as well as our observations – demonstrate that there is a clear line of sight between a lack of theological knowledge and influence among the board of trustees and a loss of an organisation's Christian identity and purpose.

To state it plainly, Christian organisations need trustees and directors who have theological credentials in their governance structures.

11. Leadership transition

Renewal is a good and necessary thing, and that is true at the board and trustee level as much as the executive level of the organisation. New leadership brings fresh eyes and new energy which can invigorate the organisation.

However, with such change also comes challenges and risk. At the trustee and director level, there is the danger that those new board members, consciously or unconsciously, try to assimilate the Christian organisation to the norms and practices and approaches that are common within their spheres of competence and experience, rather than the other way round. They fail to appreciate the operational implications that come from the fact that the objective of this Christian organisation is to seek to fulfil God's mission on earth, not property, finance or marketing outcomes.

The same is true for the appointment of a new CEO or senior executives. Is the recruitment process focusing on someone whose passion is to participate in God's mission? Or is it focusing on something else? Please don't misunderstand us: we are not endorsing the appointment of incompetent believers! Skills are essential, so it isn't an 'either/or'.

The peril of losing organisational faithfulness as a result of leadership change at the trustee, director or executive level, is the reason why the shape and content of the onboarding of new board members and executives is such a mission-critical task. Our observation is that sadly too often, such orientation is focused on what the organisation does and where it does it; what shape the finances are in and what its strategy for the future is. Too often, the identity and purpose of the organisation is taken as a given, and there is no discussion of how the 'Who?' and 'Why?' shapes the 'What?' and 'How?'

12. God's airtime

One indication of whether faithfulness is being lost is seen in what boards and the executive spend their time considering at their meetings. Too often such meetings begin with a perfunctory prayer – and then the rest of the meeting is dominated by more pressing matters such as finance, property, legal and compliance matters. This infers that the meeting has quickly moved to the comfort zones of its members. Any semblance of concern for identity and purpose – discerning God's will and putting it into practice – has been supplanted by a preoccupation with the activity itself.

There are ways to push back against this propensity to focus on activity rather than purpose. The first place to start is with the agenda. Too often, agendas are heavily influenced by executives who might need board approval for such matters as spending money on IT systems or property. Boards or individual directors who are determined to maintain a focus on organisational faithfulness need to seize back their meeting agendas from the pressing needs of executives. They can ensure that time is spent on considering and directing faithfulness issues.

What the board spends its time on will reveal to the entire organisation what board members really consider important. Is time spent on organisational faithfulness issues? Or how its Christian identity and purpose flow through to its strategy, staff issues and financial considerations? If that is a preoccupation of governance meetings, it will also become a primary concern for the organisation as a whole.[19]

The same applies to executive leadership meetings. If these meetings are preoccupied with the 'What?', 'How?' and 'When?', and there is a paucity of reflection on Christian identity and purpose, we should not then be surprised if issues to do with purpose are perceived to be tangential by the rest of the organisation's staff.

13. Your community of interest

As we mentioned earlier, most Christian organisations were founded with a strong and close-knit 'community of interest'. But as these organisations develop and grow, there is a tendency for that community of interest to dissipate. Members of the founding group step back, while others step forward to take their place. There are more divergent voices, different opinions, and various traditions and backgrounds.

Such developments bring much good. The organisation is refreshed, younger people are introduced into the leadership of the organisation, the skills and expertise among the trustees or directors – and within the organisation – are drawn from a wider group. Atrophy and staleness are avoided.

However, there are also downsides. Shared perspectives are diluted as the leadership is drawn from a broader group. Different views on how God works in creation and what roles his disciples play may begin to become apparent. There may not be agreement on the approach to finance, or risk, or grace, or other elements of an organisational theology we mentioned earlier. And, in an absence of actions that come from a shared faith, we wind up with activity without foundations.

---

19 See Garratt, *The Fish Rots from the Head*. Note: chapter 1, 'Directing not Managing', sets out the issues well.

How do you know whether an organisation has a community of interest? How do you know whether it is based on theological grounds? One way to test this is to suggest or commence the development of a Statement of Organisational Theology upon which to base critical decisions. The reactions to such an activity may range from enthusiasm to hesitancy, awkwardness or downright hostility. Each of these responses will indicate whether a community of interest exists and, if it does, whether its basis is faithful or functional, and purposive or practical.

14. Disengagement from churches

Many Christian organisations that were established with complete independence from any church denomination. We have already mentioned examples of these: Habitat for Humanity, World Vision, Mission Australia, Opportunity International and Compassion have all been established as separate entities from denominations, even though they are fulfilling activities that are important expressions of Christian discipleship.

At the same time, there have been some organisations whose origins are denominational but have subsequently sought to distance themselves – in brand, governance and influence – from the churches that founded them.[20] There are a variety of reasons for this independence. Some sought to reach beyond denominational divides for their support; others did not want to be constrained by the strictures of denominational governance.

However, in a post-Christian world, we need to think again. Few independent 'Christian organisations' have maintained their Christian identity, motivation and purpose for more than 70 or 80 years. Instead, as Peter Greer observes: 'Wisdom lies in anchoring ourselves to the church as the church is anchored to Christ. Across time and culture and trends, the church remains.'[21]

20 Judd, Robinson & Errington, *Driven by Purpose*, pp. 93–94, 138.
21 Greer & Horst, *Mission Drift*, p. 173.

Let us hasten to add that we are not suggesting that such independent organisations somehow fold into a denomination and become subject to their governance structures! They do not have to lose their independence. However, in the 21st century 'independence' has become an existential exposure for Christian organisations. There is no-one to keep these organisations 'honest' in terms of their organisational faithfulness.

And when it comes to an external review of its organisational faithfulness, the suggestion is rarely warmly embraced by any Christian organisation. As Burtchaell tartly observed, perhaps with hyperbole, the Christian universities he researched were more likely to report to 'the federal government how many students of Samoan extraction they enroll' than report how faithfully they were serving the Christian communities that founded them.[22]

Such external accountability of organisational faithfulness rightly imports into the organisational and corporate realm the many biblical injunctions for individual Christians to be accountable to each other.[23] For this reason, Christian organisations need to develop models where they engage external analysts and reviewers, people who are aligned with the organisation's theology and framework and who can be critical friends: engaging, challenging and encouraging the organisation in its faithfulness.

How does your organisation rate?

It is one thing to do a self-analysis, but the following review questions – discussed with key leaders in the organisation – will help you be more confident of where your organisation stands.

---

22 Burtchaell, *The Dying of the Light*, p. 834.
23 1 Cor 5:6; Eph 4:15, 25; Rom 14:13ff; Gal 6:1–2.

Review questions

1. Chris Crane of Edify says that it is the natural evolution of many originally Christ-centred missions is to drift. Can you think of examples of this? What do you understand were the circumstances?

2. In this chapter we maintain that a loss of faithfulness is always gradual and subtle. Do you agree?

3. In this chapter we looked at some of the ways that organisational faithfulness is lost. These include:

   - the presence of hubris
   - the hoax of harmony
   - strategies that leave purpose behind.

   Are any of these dangers likely to be in an organisation that you are familiar with?

4. Do donors impact on an organisation's faithfulness? How can this be addressed? Do you have any examples of how this was resolved?

5. How do government regulators impact on an organisation's faithfulness, if at all? How can that challenge be countered?

6. In this chapter we noted the apparent anticlericalism that was present in organisations that experienced mission drift. Why do you think this is so? How might this be remedied? What are the benefits of the contribution of those with theological qualifications?

7. A strong community of interest is a key hallmark of an organisation that is faithful. How might such a community be preserved, encouraged and maintained?

8. Peter Greer says that 'Wisdom lies in anchoring ourselves to the church as the church is anchored to Christ. Across time and culture and trends,

the church remains.' Do you agree with Greer? What are some other ways that Christian organisations might have such an anchor?

9. In this chapter we suggested that along with external auditors of organisational finances or consultants who review risk management or governance, Christian organisations should have external reviewers of how they are organisationally faithful. Do you agree? Give reasons for your response.

Everything is possible with God

Christian charity has been attributed with changing the world. It transformed the Roman Empire: by 250 CE the Christian community in Rome was supporting 1,500 poor people each and every day.[1] This organised activity was completely counter to the prevailing Graeco-Roman culture, within which it was anathema to love the poor, the sick, the orphaned or the widowed. However, Christians didn't stop there. Later, in the centuries that followed, Christians established countless organisations to care for the sick and dying; provide for the orphans and widows; meet the welfare needs of the hungry, the poor and the homeless; and educate the young. Such organised Christian activity became a distinctive and transformative hallmark of the societies wherever Christians were found. Make no mistake: over two millennia these health, welfare and educational initiatives were overwhelmingly founded by Christians, not pagan or secular groups.

The reason this was the case was that Christian corporate activity was founded on the thoroughly revolutionary understanding that God's love for humankind was an impetus for action by those claiming Christ's name.

However, if the establishment of these Christian organisations was motivated by and reflective of God's love, and if these organisations have collectively been such an integral part of the fabric of society, it is all the more sobering to acknowledge that over the years so many of these organisations

---

1 See Dickson, *The Best Kept Secret*, ch. 6.

have lost their Christian identity. The annals of history are pockmarked with organisations that were established by faithful Christians to serve their fellow men and women as they sought to partner with God to bring in his kingdom – and then they slowly and inexorably lost their faithfulness, embracing humanist values. Founded with Christian zeal, passion and daring entrepreneurialism, these organisations flourished for a season or three and then withered, their Christian drive and motivation replaced by a mechanistic focus on activity and confusion regarding their mission or purpose.

The responsibility for this slide lies at the feet of the believers involved in these organisations and no-one else. Yet, these Christian trustees, board members and executives responsible for the dissolution of their organisation's identity didn't wake up one morning and intentionally decide to undermine the Christian character of the organisation. Rather, they were blind to the consequences of their actions. Even so, such cognitive blindness is sinful, because the decisions that have been made and the actions that have been taken have lacked any grounding in the mind of Christ.

If you can't see something, then you can't address it. People find themselves living in systems of sin without knowing that they are doing so. In this way we can talk about sin as being systemic. It becomes a shared illusion within which certain things are assumed to be fine, which they are if you are inside the system and sharing in the illusion. However, those on the outside looking in can see that something is seriously wrong. We have given various examples of how this works itself out in the life of Christian organisations. The prophetic task of those who work both with and in Christian organisations is to reveal systems of sin and raise people's awareness of the illusions in which they are caught up, in order that organisations can behave in ways that are more faithful to God.

A central theme of this book is that most Christian organisations have less secure Christ-centred foundations than they would like to believe.

This is because there is no connection between the varied beliefs of the individuals who serve within these organisations and their corporate action. If God's wisdom is 'a practical knowledge of how to act well, grounded in the reality of the world God has made' then a failure to bridge this gap is certainly foolishness.[2]

We have suggested that an articulated organisational theology is a necessary way to bridge that gap by taking the shared beliefs of God and seeking, however imperfectly, to make it a lived experience for all parts of the organisation and its endeavours. It is the way to transform belief into an organisation's lived experience of faith – what we have called 'organisational faithfulness'. When the organisation starts thinking about how belief is transformed into practice, the journey becomes as important as the destination as people have the opportunity to continually reflect on how they honour their God in practice.

Matthew records these words of Jesus:

> You are the salt of the earth. But if the salt loses its saltiness, how can it be made salty again? It is no longer good for anything, except to be thrown out and trampled underfoot.

> You are the light of the world. A town built on a hill cannot be hidden. Neither do people light a lamp and put it under a bowl. Instead they put it on its stand, and it gives light to everyone in the house. In the same way, let your light shine before others, that they may see your good deeds and glorify your Father in heaven (Matt 5:13–16).

Jesus' words are both an inspiration and a warning, not just for individual believers but for organisations that claim to follow him. For centuries, Christian organisations have experienced a slide into secularism which has only become obvious in hindsight.

---

2 Errington, *Every Good Path*, p. 3.

However, it need not be like that. We have identified how and when this drift can occur, and we have suggested some ways to arrest or avoid the slide so that Christian organisations can continue to show God's love for his creation.

Some readers might think the task of maintaining organisational faithfulness is too hard. There is no doubt that it requires conscious effort and hard work. However, if we are serious in our claim to be followers of Jesus in our collective activity, then faith is key. As the writer of the Hebrews puts it: 'faith is confidence in what we hope for and assurance about what we do not see' (Heb 11:1). We are not called to be successful, lauded, powerful or all-conquering ... We are simply called to be faithful.

BIBLIOGRAPHY

Braithwaite, John, Braithwaite, Valerie, and Makkai, Toni. *Regulating Aged Care*, Eerdmans, London, 2007.

Buechner, Frederick. *Beyond Words*, Harper, New York, 2004.

Burtchaell, James Tunstead. *The Dying of the Light: The Disengagement of Colleges and Universities from their Christian Churches*, Eerdmans, Grand Rapids MI, 1998.

Dickson, John. *The Best Kept Secret of Christian Mission*, Zondervan, Grand Rapids MI, 2010.

Eastman, Susan Grove. 'The "Empire of Illusion": Sin, Evil, and Good News in Romans', in *Comfortable Words: Essays in Honor of Paul F.M. Zahl*, eds. John Koch and Todd Brewer, Wipf & Stock, Eugene OR, 2013.

Errington, Andrew. *Every Good Path: Wisdom and Practical Reason in Christian Ethics and the Book of Proverbs*, T&T Clark, London, 2020.

Garratt, Bob. *The Fish Rots from the Head*, Harper Collins, London, 1997.

Greer, Peter, and Horst, Chris. *Mission Drift*, Bethany House, Bloomington MN, 2014.

Hedges, Chris. *Empire of Illusion*, Bold Type Books, New York, 2009.

Judd, Stephen, and Robinson, Anne. 'Christianity and social services in Australia', in Piggin, Stuart (Ed.). *Shaping the Good Society in Australia*, Australia's Christian Heritage National Forum, 2006, pp. 109–125.

Judd, Stephen, Robinson, Anne, and Errington, Felicity. *Driven by Purpose: Charities That Make the Difference*, HammondPress, Sydney, 2012.

Lake, Meredith. *Faith in Action*, UNSW Press, Sydney, 2013.

Lewis, C.S. *Mere Christianity*, HarperOne, San Francisco, 2016 [1952].

Marsden, George. *The Soul of the American University: From Protestant Establishment to Established Non-belief*, Oxford University Press, New York, 1994.

Sacks, Jonathan. *The Politics of Hope*, Jonathan Cape, London, 1997.

Sinek, Simon. *Start with Why*, Penguin, London, 2009.

Sproul, R.C. *Everyone's a Theologian*, Reformation Trust, Sanford FL, 2014.

Vanhoozer, Kevin J. *The Drama of Doctrine: A Canonical Linguistic Approach to Christian Doctrine*, Westminster John Knox Press, Louisville KY, 2005.

Risk Management Policy of the Church Missionary Society of Australia

The content below is reproduced with permission of CMS-A.[1]

Risk Management Policy

Purpose

To describe CMS-A approach to risk, and to set out the framework for managing risk.

Definition

Assessed Risk: Risks assessed by Board/Management before any controls are put in place.

Residual Risk: Risks after Board/Management has put in place controls to manage these risks.

Theology of Risk

Our understanding and management of risk is based on a theology of the sovereign God deploying his witnesses in a risky world, until Jesus returns.

The sovereignty of God

We believe that the Lord Jesus Christ is the great Shepherd of his sheep. We entrust ourselves to the care of the Master Shepherd, confident of our Lord's loving kindness, covenant faithfulness and sovereign rule over all our lives.

---

1 Our thanks to Peter Rodgers, federal secretary, and Geoff Girvan, federal treasurer, of CMS-A for making this excerpt of the CMS-A 'Risk Management Policy' available and for discussing its implementation.

The great commissioning of God

God sends his Word into his world on the lips and in the lives of his children, to make disciples from all peoples. God's children bear witness to the peoples of our world by proclaiming and living the cross of our Lord Jesus Christ. God's great commission is therefore a call to costly and sacrificial witness.

Security and risk

We live in a world that has rebelled against the rule of its Creator. All humanity suffers the consequence of sin resulting in the breakdown of relationship and the cascade of evil actions of men and women. Creation itself is broken, with natural disasters and catastrophic events the result. God's children are not immune from the risks of living in this broken world.

Spiritual warfare

Christians share the good news of Christ conscious that Satan is seeking to destroy the church and its testimony. Christians can expect to experience spiritual attacks and oppression. Some cultures and contexts bring this into heightened awareness impacting spiritual, psychological and physical well-being.

Courage and wise judgement

Recognising that we live in an insecure world, we trust our Heavenly Father to give us courage in the face of fear. We pray for wisdom that we might live both confidently and prudently in the face of many risks. As God graciously gives us his Word, his courage and his wisdom, he enables us through the power of his Spirit to make wise choices that avoid on the one hand foolhardiness or recklessness, and on the other hand undue fear and anxiety.

Human frailty, prayer and God's providence

Acknowledging our human frailty and limited understanding, we are bound to be imperfect in our knowledge, decisions and actions. In humble but bold confidence, we pray to God to guide us in all we do, trusting his promises to guide us in right paths that bring glory to him, even amidst the fallenness of humanity.

Our secure hope

Our hope in Christ is never at risk. We live and serve in this world in the sure knowledge of our salvation and in the power of his Holy Spirit. We eagerly look forward to the return of Christ when he will judge evil, establish his kingdom, and take us to our perfect and eternal home kept safe for us in heaven.

Submission to authority

God has established the ruler and authorities and we submit to these authorities, ensuring compliance in all relevant secular laws.

Acknowledgements

The authors would like to acknowledge contributions from the following individuals and organisations:

Geoff Girvan and Peter Rodgers of the Church Missionary Society of Australia and Tracey West of Interserve for sharing how theology shaped their respective organisations' thinking about risk and its management.

Dr Tim Wright, formerly Head of The Shore School, Sydney for sharing his experiences of the application of Christian ideals within a school community.

Emeritus Professor John Clark and Revd Dr Andrew Judd for reading an early draft of one chapter and making incisive observations.

Professor John Dickson for his historical observations, not least the examples of the gap between belief and behaviour.

Peter Greer, who co-authored in 2014 with Chris Horst *Mission Drift: The Unspoken Crisis Facing Leaders, Charities and Churches*, for sharing so many insights and observations.

Our many work colleagues and friends, most of whom prefer to be unnamed, who gave examples of how Christian organisations wrestle with faithfulness, too often without success. And to John Nadjarian, who was, quite typically, willing to be named!

Our warm thanks also to Bible Society Australia, Owen Salter and Kris Argall for their editing suggestions, and Simon Smart for his enthusiastic support of this project.

May these words of our hands and these meditations of our hearts be pleasing in your sight, Lord Jesus, our Rock and our Redeemer (Ps 19:14).

www.ingramcontent.com/pod-product-compliance
Lightning Source LLC
Chambersburg PA
CBHW062110080426
42734CB00012B/2812